Tanja Fuß

NEGOTIATIONS WITH THE JAPANESE

Overcoming Intercultural Communication Hurdles

AUSSENHANDELSPOLITIK UND -PRAXIS

Herausgegeben von Prof. Dr. Jörn Altmann

ISSN 1614-3582

1 *Anja Marx*
  Außenhandel mit Italien
  Ein Exportratgeber für deutsche Unternehmen
  ISBN 3-89821-072-3

2 *Quynh Anh Dang*
  Foreign Direct Investment in Vietnam
  Chancen und Risiken für ausländische Investoren im vietnamesischen Markt
  ISBN 3-89821-260-2

3 *Jürgen Neuberger*
  Gesellschaftsformen in Europa und den USA im Vergleich
  ISBN 3-89821-311-0

4 *Thomas Steffen*
  Japan im Wandel
  Chancen, Risiken und Erfolgsfaktoren für ausländische Unternehmen
  ISBN 3-89821-298-X

5 *Thomas Wölfel*
  Marken- und Produktpiraterie
  Eine Studie zu Erscheinungsformen und Bekämpfungsmöglichkeiten
  ISBN 3-89821-284-X

6 *Imke Heinrich*
  Markenführung als strategischer Erfolgsfaktor
  ISBN 3-89821-351-X

7 *Albrecht Neumann*
  Kulturspezifische Probleme in deutsch-russischen Wirtschaftsbeziehungen
  Das Beispiel Siemens Business Services in Moskau
  ISBN 3-89821-408-7

8 *Tanja Fuß*
  Negotiations with the Japanese
  Overcoming Intercultural Communication Hurdles
  ISBN 3-89821-420-6

Tanja Fuß

NEGOTIATIONS WITH THE JAPANESE

Overcoming Intercultural Communication Hurdles

ibidem-Verlag
Stuttgart

Bibliografische Information Der Deutschen Bibliothek

Die Deutsche Bibliothek verzeichnet diese Publikation in der Deutschen Nationalbibliografie; detaillierte bibliografische Daten sind im Internet über <http://dnb.ddb.de> abrufbar.

Gedruckt auf alterungsbeständigem, säurefreien Papier
Printed on acid-free paper

ISSN: 1614-3582
ISBN: 3-89821-420-6

© *ibidem*-Verlag
Stuttgart 2005
Alle Rechte vorbehalten

Das Werk einschließlich aller seiner Teile ist urheberrechtlich geschützt. Jede Verwertung außerhalb der engen Grenzen des Urheberrechtsgesetzes ist ohne Zustimmung des Verlages unzulässig und strafbar. Dies gilt insbesondere für Vervielfältigungen, Übersetzungen, Mikroverfilmungen und elektronische Speicherformen sowie die Einspeicherung und Verarbeitung in elektronischen Systemen.

Printed in Germany

Outline

1 Introduction 7
  1.1 Motivation 7
  1.2 Objectives and approach 10
  1.3 Framework for intercultural business negotiations 13
2 Main part 19
  2.1 Theory 19
    2.1.1 Culture and cultural dimensions 19
      2.1.1.1 Power distance 23
      2.1.1.2 Individualism and collectivism 26
      2.1.1.3 Masculinity and femininity 31
      2.1.1.4 Uncertainty avoidance 34
      2.1.1.5 Long term orientation and time perception 37
    2.1.2 Language, communication and information exchange 41
      2.1.2.1 Language 41
      2.1.2.2 Paraverbal and non-verbal communication 47
      2.1.2.3 Information flow 49
    2.1.3 Working ethics and ideals 51
      2.1.3.1 Education and career in Japan 51
      2.1.3.2 Leadership and motivation 58
      2.1.3.3 Hierarchy and formality 60
      2.1.3.4 Decision making and responsibility 64
      2.1.3.5 Negotiating 66
      2.1.3.6 Legal conception and conflict solving 69

2.2 Case Studies 75

    2.2.1 Penetrating group structures 75
    2.2.2 Relationship orientation versus uncertainty avoidance 77
    2.2.3 Consideration interpreted as criticism 80
    2.2.4 Conflict management 82
    2.2.5 Priority Japan: Product trademarks 86
    2.2.6 Saying "yes, but…" instead of "no" 88
    2.2.7 A Japanese management tool in a German organization 90
    2.2.8 Expressing individual opinion 93
    2.2.9 Possible to know is need to know 97
    2.2.10 Politics in business 100
    2.2.11 Foreigners and in-groups 103

3   Conclusion 107

    3.1 Coping with cultural differences 107

    3.2 Creating cultural synergies 111

    3.3 Summary 114

4   Indices 117

    4.1 Literature 117

    4.2 Index of tables 122

    4.3 Index of figures 122

    4.4 Japanese terms 123

1 Introduction
1.1 Motivation

Japan is the second largest economic power in the world after the USA.[1] At the same time, it is probably the culture the most foreign to the other large economic powers of the world, which are, with the exception of the Russian Federation, all Western countries.

Japan's economic development, its modernity and degree of industrialization may lead to the assumption that there are no major differences in the Japanese way of thinking, motivations and value system to those of Western cultures. This is a dangerous misconception.

Japan has imported many elements of Western cultures, but these elements are always only isolated segments which never form a system functioning by itself. The Japanese culture can be compared to a language with its own structure and grammar, which has adapted a lot of foreign words that are superficially recognizable to foreigners, but which have hardly touched the basic social grammar.[2] Dressing similarly, buying the same products and using the same fashionable words by no means constitutes a common culture. "These rather superficial manifestations of culture are sometimes mistaken for all there is; the deeper, underlying level of values, which moreover determine the meaning for people of their practices, is overlooked. Studies at the values level continue to show impressive differences among nations..."[3]

Japan has a long history of adopting foreign practices, symbols and views. Change is not considered negative, and seldom meets with strong resistance. However, superficial changes in attitude and behaviour hardly ever influences the invariable basic character of human relationships and group dyna-

---

[1] cf. MPHPT (2003), p. 25
[2] Nakane (1985), p. 200
[3] Hofstede (2003), p. 181

mics.[4] Rather than replacing a tradition, a new concept of acting and thinking is merely added to the existing patterns and exercised in parallel. Many experts consider it unlikely that basic cultural values will change faster than within a century timeframe.[5]

While being considered as highly westernised, Japan and Japanese behaviour is simultaneously often perceived as incomprehensibly exotic, irrational and even absurd.

There seems to be a considerable lack of information to base interpretation of Japanese behaviour on in the West. Both in literature and in the author's experience, there is a lot of potential for intercultural misunderstandings, miscommunications and problems in this lack. This is further enhanced by the Japanese inexperience in intercultural contacts. Though they tend to be more aware of (at least superficial) differences between them and Westerners, they don't seem to have developed an appropriate code of conduct for interacting with strangers, leading to considerable insecurity on their part when confronted with a foreigner.[6] Internationalisation (国際化 *kokusaika*) is an ideal highly valued in Japan, but exercising it in an island country whose recent history contains almost 300 years of total isolation from the rest of the world still happens often more in theory than in practice.

What further aggravates the situation is that it is obviously difficult to acknowledge the fact that cultural differences induce different behaviour than that one considers 'normal' at home.

> "Everybody looks at the world from behind the windows of a cultural home and everybody prefers to act as if people from other countries have something special about them (a national character) but home is normal.

---

[4] Nakane (1985), p. 199
[5] cf. Hofstede (2003), pp. 46-47
[6] Nakane (1985), pp. 176-177

Unfortunately, there is no normal position in cultural matters. This is an uncomfortable message, as uncomfortable as Galileo Galilei's claim in the seventeenth century that the Earth is not the center of the Universe."[7]

Equally unfortunately, it is obviously just as hard to believe as Galilei's finding has been to his contemporaries. Instead, when encountering unfamiliar behaviour in foreign interaction partners, many people automatically assume a fault in character as the cause, never considering that the other person might act according to a different value system, which is neither inferior nor superior to one's own.

Even for foreigners willing to accept the existence of differing cultural values, when trying to "learn" a new culture, it is not easy to discern and understand the underlying value system. "In a way, the visitor in a foreign culture returns to the mental state of an infant, in which he or she has to learn the simplest things over again. This usually leads to feelings of distress, of helplessness, and of hostility towards the new environment."[8]

It seems intercultural conflicts are inevitable in such circumstances. There are countless examples for problems in interacting with the Japanese (some of which will be included in this book, see chapter 2.2) which have merely arisen for cultural reasons. In fact, problems of intercultural communication and adaptation are the main cause for Western expatriates prematurely leaving Japan.[9] To the author's knowledge, there are no statistics on the relation between failure of international negotiations and intercultural misunderstandings. But in her more than ten years of experience in Japanese-Western

---

[7] Hofstede (2003), p. 235
[8] Hofstede (2003), p. 209
[9] cf. Kühlmann (1995), pp. 2-...?:

business relations, almost every major conflict encountered could be traced down to cultural rather than personal or factual reasons.

This is at once unsettling and encouraging. Unsettling, because there is obviously a lot of completely unnecessary conflict. Encouraging, because it can be avoided by the appropriate preparation of intercultural contacts. And even in case misunderstandings have already occurred, they can frequently be resolved through clarifying communication and adaptation of behaviour.[10]
After all, as opposed to conflicts related to factual differences, culture-based conflicts are neither necessary nor usually wanted by the parties involved, and thus avoiding them is to the benefit of everyone.

1.2 Objectives and approach

This book pursues three major objectives.

First, the characteristics of Japanese culture and their differences from Western cultures shall be described, **identifying potential sources of conflict**. The focus will lie on characteristics relevant for business contacts and negotiations.

These descriptions will be supported by a number of practical examples, all of which have been taken from the author's own experience in dealing with Japanese interaction partners. By supplementing theory with practice, it will become more obvious to the reader how situations that merely seem strange to the average Westerner can be **analysed for underlying cultural values** with the appropriate knowledge.

Finally, the book will present various ways of coping with intercultural complications and **solving conflicts**, as well as avoiding conflicts altogether and making use of possible cross-cultural synergies.

---

[10] cf. Dülfer (1996), p. 387

This book is not intended to be an instruction manual on how to behave in Japan: there will be no information on how to use chopsticks or hand over business cards or on the appropriate angle of bowing when meeting a superior. It is meant to enable the reader to analyse situations, to sensitise him for possible causes of conflict, and to impart enough knowledge about the Japanese culture for him to act and communicate successfully in Japan. However, one has to keep in mind that there are no standard situations: "It has been stated many times that each cross-cultural relationship is not only a complex situation, it is also a unique situation which has to be understood individually in each case."[11] However, for describing a supposedly homogeneous culture and its characteristics, as well as its variances from other supposedly homogeneous cultures, some general assumptions have to be made. Therefore, this book will contain generalizations like 'the Japanese' and 'the Westerners', pretending there is any such thing as a typical member of a culture behaving in a predictably typical way.

Particularly, the reader should keep in mind that some of the assumptions concerning working life and ideals are only true for large Japanese enterprises and their permanent employees. However, these are probably the negotiation partners he is most likely to encounter.

Generally, the point of view the book assumes will be that of a Western member of an organisation or company negotiating with his Japanese counterpart. The Western negotiator is assumed to be in the weaker position (e.g. a vendor trying to convince a customer of his products), so he is forced to comply with the Japanese cultural requirements to some extent.

---

[11] Gullestrup (2003/2004), p. 15

Negotiation, in this book, is understood in a very wide sense, not restricting the term to formal meetings with an agenda and professional negotiators. Rather, negotiation is considered to happen whenever people communicate in order to achieve a certain result or target.[12] As stated before, the focus of the book lies on business life, so the negotiation targets tend to be business-related. No special attention will be dedicated to political negotiation, although of course many statements are equally applicable to business and political negotiation situations.

What is not part of this book is researching the reasons for cultural differences and characteristics. Occasionally these may be briefly touched upon, but they will not even constitute a side issue, as the topic is much too complex and requires a totally different approach (plus much more space than available here).

Equally, there will be no information regarding sub-cultures or local cultures. For the sake of generalization, one more or less homogeneous Japanese culture is assumed.

Finally, clarification is required on what is actually meant by "Western". The countries that have been by arbitrary definition of the author included in this term are Northern America, Western Europe (excluding Turkey and Eastern Europe), and Australia. Still, there almost certainly will be a bias towards Germany, the USA and the UK, these being the cultures the author has most experience with apart from Japan.

---

[12] cf. Gaspardo (2000), p. 3

1.3 Framework for intercultural business negotiations

There are various situational contexts in which negotiations between Westerners and Japanese can occur. As stated before, the weaker position will be assumed for the Western negotiator, so situations in which the Japanese would have to adapt to the Westerner's requirements are deliberately left out in the following.

One large group of negotiation situations is communication between people working together for the same company or organisation. This can happen in several variations:

First, one can be assigned to Japan as an employee of a foreign company's subsidiary. Usually, this happens to managers or technical experts. Both will be highly dependent not only on the co-operation of their colleagues for succeeding in their business target, but also on their help for mastering daily life an a country as foreign as Japan. Especially if they do not speak the language, simple tasks like buying a train ticket or ordering food in a restaurant can be hard to accomplish. Moreover, the foreigner is removed from his social environment and may experience a considerable culture shock, which further complicates successful communication with the Japanese especially in the early phases of the assignment.

Usually, there are four phases to acculturation for expatriates in a foreign country: the first is termed euphoria or honeymoon, as in the beginning of the stay, the country and culture is regarded in a similar way as when travelling for tourism: only the positive, exciting and curious aspects are realized. This usually short phase is followed by culture shock, when the visitor realizes that the differences he experienced so far are only the surface of a completely different value system, and that he doesn't have enough information to judge or predict even basic situations. In the third phase, acculturation sets in as the foreigner gradually learns the rules of his new environment, and becomes more and more integrated. Phase 4 is the stable state or balance reached after the ups and downs experienced in the previous phases.[13]

Even if there is preparation regarding intercultural differences prior to the assignment, many expatriates state that they only realized their full scope and impact after arriving in Japan.[14]

Paradoxically, in an environment so full of rules of conduct enforced by social expectation, many foreigners experience exactly the opposite: not being a member of any ingroup, but an exotic outsider, any kind of behaviour is expected from them, and many of their actions (though unfortunately not those offending a subconscious value) are excused by the fact that they are 変な外人 *henna gaijin*, "strange foreigners".[15] If they happen to act conforming to existing rules, the Japanese often seem more surprised than pleased, or they react over-enthusiastic to the most basic adaptations in behaviour. One German expatriate complained that after almost 30 years living in Japan, he still received compliments on how good he was with chopsticks, which he felt to be a quite frustrating hint that he still was an outsider.

In the case of a manager being assigned to Japan with the task of managing Japanese employees, there are some more special circumstances which may endanger successful interaction with the Japanese. (This case is included here, as the foreign superior of Japanese employees is, though not as a rule in a weaker position, in a state of dependency, as his success hinges on the performance of his subordinates.)

The foreign superior's responsibility includes leadership and personnel management tasks like motivating his employees, integrating them within

---

[13] Hofstede (2003), pp. 209-210
[14] cf. Dülfer (1996), pp. 178-179
[15] cf. Thomas (2001), p. 12

the company structure, familiarizing them with the corporate goals and strategies and ensuring adequate internal communication.[16] These tasks require a high skill in personal interaction, and are extremely difficult to accomplish when lacking knowledge on what is socially desirable behaviour. Many personnel management tools and methods that work in the West have to be abandoned, and soft skills must be acquired anew under different circumstances.

One more difficulty to overcome is that even if the manager knows what would be best in a certain situation, often he cannot act accordingly, as he has to represent the interests and carry out the directives of his parent company. The headquarters, however important one single subsidiary may be, will always make their decisions from the point of view of the whole enterprise, which frequently does not take into account the special circumstances and necessities of local markets. So the expatriate manager will sometimes have to enforce decisions which he himself does not identify with, and which may be harmful from an intercultural relations point of view.[17]

When working for a Japanese organisation in a Western country, the situation is somewhat different. First, one remains within one's familiar social environment. Usually, there will be many other foreign (i.e. non-Japanese) employees in a foreign subsidiary. Western labour laws apply, so the working conditions will be equal or at least very similar to what one is used to from working for a Western company. Last but not least, the Japanese expatriates assigned to a foreign country will in most cases arrive with a minimum of preparation, knowing they're expected to behave differently than in Japan.

Still, when working with Japanese colleagues, working for a Japanese superior or even managing Japanese employees, it is crucial to understand the

---

[16] cf. Dülfer (1996), pp. 40-41
[17] cf. Dülfer (1996), p. 390

differences in value systems between Japan and the West. This knowledge can help avoid many a misunderstanding or conflict, and thus save considerable time, effort and money for the company.

When working for the same organisation, especially in Japan, one might expect that just by being a member of it, one becomes a member of the same in-group as one's colleagues. It is true that through this automatic relationship, including an identifiable hierarchical position, access to Japan is somewhat facilitated. But group members are expected to display behaviour conform to the group's formal and informal rules. Infringing those rules too often, no matter if deliberately or by ignorance, means endangering one's position in the group by showing one is an outsider.

The other large group of negotiation situations happens between members of different organizations. Here the variety of negotiation partners is greater, ranging from administrative authorities through suppliers and distributors, investors and banks to (potential) customers.
In all of these negotiation situations, the Westerner is to some extent in the weaker position, having to adapt to Japanese cultural standards in order to be successful.
Authorities in Japan are used to being paid a lot of respect, and are known to be not very flexible. When confronted with foreigners, civil servants tend to react with insecurity or suspicion.[18] In many cases, foreigners are required to have a Japanese warrantor to obtain certain rights (like renting an apartment or establishing a company).
If a conflict with the authorities arises, it is generally advisable to involve a Japanese mediator who aids the negotiations, ideally one with an existing

---

[18] cf. Thomas (2001), p. 250

relationship to the civil servant (e.g. a graduate from the same university).[19] The solution of the conflict, however, will always be a compromise, as the authority would lose face if they revised a decision once made.

Banks are to some extent similar to authorities, being very bureaucratic and demanding a high level of security in the form of warrantors and transparent and abundant information. Shareholders, traditionally, used to have a somewhat weaker position than e.g. in the USA. Due to international competition on the financial markets and through several reforms of laws regulating investors' rights, however, this is rapidly changing. Shareholders now have extensive information access rights, and Japanese companies are discovering them as a new target group to be treated with the same courtesy and care as customers.[20]

Suppliers and distributors are usually not in a stronger negotiating position compared to their contracting company. However, in Japan, most of these companies are integrated in a tight network of relationships which is hard to penetrate for a foreign enterprise. So it may happen that the Western negotiator trying to enter the Japanese market is actually dependent on the distributor's or supplier's readiness to co-operate.

There is a saying in Japan stating that "the customer is god", underlining the importance to maintain good relationships with any customer at all costs. "When it comes to customer demands, the unreasonable is reasonable. One Japanese said, "In the U.S. the customer-vendor relationship is a partnership. In Japan, it is an ownership.""[21] Customers are used to be treated with prior-

---

[19] cf. Thomas (2001), p. 250
[20] cf. Nakamura (2001), pp. 1-4
[21] Gundling (1999), p. 16

ity over everything else, and to have their requests fulfilled by their vendors, however difficult they may be. Vendors put massive effort in complying with their customer's wishes, as they know that they are sure to be rewarded with future business opportunities by the satisfied customer.[22]

In any case the negotiator, whether he is dependent on his Japanese negotiation partner or in a stronger position, can immensely increase the success of the negotiation by being aware of cultural differences as sources of misunderstandings.
The next chapter will look at basic principles of culture, and in particular at the characteristics of the Japanese culture compared to the West.

---

[22] Gundling (1999), p. 17

2 Main part
2.1 Theory
2.1.1 Culture and cultural dimensions

Culture is a term which cannot easily be defined. Most people associate music, literature and fine arts with the term, plus maybe historic buildings or artisan products that are considered typical for any given local culture. More internationally experienced persons may count foreign customs and behaviours differing from what is standard at their home country among what constitutes culture.

And even when reading guidebooks for travellers and businessmen, one gets the impression that a foreign culture consists of not much more than different rituals for greeting and variances in eating manners.

These aspects of culture, of course, are not to be neglected, as they are indeed the visible and explicit manifestations of a culture. Yet, culture consists of many more layers that are not as obvious, and these 'invisible' but immensely powerful factors are what influences the behaviour of every member of the respective culture every day, in ways which are mostly not conscious and therefore all the more influential.

When encountering a member of an unfamiliar culture, "not every observation is decisive for the understanding of the culture. Some, especially the immediately "visible" cultural traits, may only be an expression, or symbol or symptom, of the more fundamental cultural traits, such as attitudes and values. At the same time they may - and usually do - have importance for the cultural understanding within themselves. It is therefore meaningful to talk about a hierarchy of observations - a vertical cultural dimension - in which a deeper penetration from the "immediately observable symbols" to the "fundamental legitimating values" and the "fundamental philosophy of life" will create a continuously deeper insight into the culture observed."[23]

Geert Hofstede defines values, the most basic layer of culture, as "broad tendencies to prefer certain states of affairs over others"[24], such as good over evil or rational over irrational. These preferences are acquired at a very early age, through education, social environment and personal experiences[25], and are therefore deeply rooted in the subconscious of each culture's members, influencing the way they think and act and also how they judge other people's behaviour.

Of course, these values, just like their visible expressions, can differ from person to person within a culture. The cultural environment in which they are acquired, however influential it may be, is not absolutely compelling. There is no such thing as 'the typical Japanese', 'the typical American' or 'the typical French'.

> "The *culture* of a country [...] is not a combination of properties of the 'average citizen', nor a 'modal personality'. It is, among other things, a set of likely reactions of citizens with a common mental programming. [...] Such reactions need not be found within the same *persons*, but only statistically more often in the same *society*."[26]

Likewise, there are certain motivators, needs and driving factors that all human beings share, regardless of the culture they grew up in.

> "Culture should be distinguished from human nature on one side, and from an individual's personality on the other [...], although exactly where the borders lie between human nature and culture, and between culture and personality, is a matter of discussion among social scientists."[27]

---

[23] Gullestrup (2003/2004), pp. 11-12
[24] Hofstede (2003), p. 8
[25] cf. Hofstede (2003), p. 5
[26] Hofstede (2003), p. 112
[27] Hofstede (2003), p. 5

However, for the sake of comparison, certain generalizations have to be made within this book (as stated in chapter 1.2). So both human nature and individual personality will be mostly neglected in favour of describing the 'typical' cultural values and the 'typical' behaviour they tend to induce.

Values and value systems differ from culture to culture, although of course a great deal of overlap can occur in any two cultures, either through a shared history or through mere coincidence. Both different and shared values, however, are not immediately obvious to someone not familiar with the respective culture. As long as values are congruent in the visitor's culture and the culture he/she visits, there will be hardly any problems at all, and both parties will likely not even become aware of the fact that they are sharing a common a value, as the induced behaviour will be simply taken for 'natural'. But as soon as they differ, the visitor will encounter difficulties, and the more they differ, the less he/she will be able to act, decide, solve problems or negotiate in the way he is accustomed to.

The "degree of strangeness" of a culture is the subjective lack of information on which a decision-maker will base actions and decisions, resulting from his inability to discern the effects of his environment in the consequences of his decisions, as he is not able to correctly interpret the related elements of his environment.[28]

Japan, from a Western perspective, is certainly attributed a high degree of strangeness, and therefore presents a difficult environment for the unprepared Westerner for making decisions and taking actions. Without being aware of the values influencing the Japanese behaviour, it is very easy to get lost in this foreign environment.

---

[28] cf. Dülfer (1996), p. 180

In the following, some fundamental dimensions of cultural values that occur in Japan will be described, based on findings by Geert Hofstede.[29]

Hofstede has carried out thorough analyses of data from a study among IBM employees worldwide. The cultural dimensions he discovered and the scores the various countries achieved in the analysis of the data must not be seen as absolute, but as comparative values, not showing how individualistic, hierarchical or masculine one single culture is in isolation, but how it is compared with all the others analysed.[30]

What has to be kept in mind as well when reading Hofstede's analysis is that he did not research the weight of each dimension relative to the others. So his results do not show if any of them prevails over the other(s).

---

[29] In the following tables quoted from Hofstede's book, all non-Western countries except Japan have been left out for conciseness.
[30] cf. Hofstede (2003), pp. 13-14

2.1.1.1 Power distance

"Power distance can [...] be defined as the extent to which the less powerful members of institutions and organizations within a country expect and accept that power is distributed unequally."[31]

The following table shows how various Western countries score compared to Japan.

Score rank	Country or region	PDI score
15/16	France	68
20	Belgium	65
24/25	Portugal	63
27/28	Greece	60
31	Spain	57
33	Japan	54
34	Italy	50
38	USA	40
39	Canada	39
41	Australia	36
42/44	Germany FR	35
42/44	Great Britain	35
45	Switzerland	34
46	Finland	33
47/48	Norway	31
47/48	Sweden	31
49	Ireland (Republic of)	28
51	Denmark	18
53	Austria	11

Table 1: Power Distance Index (PDI)
Source: Hofstede (2003), p. 26

---

[31] Hofstede (2003), pp. 27-28

Japan takes a medium position, but still scores higher than the majority of Western countries. This means that though Japan is not a country with an extreme power distance, it shows more characteristics of a high power distance culture than most of the countries it is compared with in this book. Therefore, in the following the characteristics of a high power distance culture will be described, to explain in which respects Japan is likely to differ from the West.

> „PDI [Power Distance Index] scores inform us about *dependence* relationships in a country. In small power distance countries there is limited dependence of subordinates on bosses, and a preference for consultation, that is, *interdependence* between boss and subordinate. [...] In large power distance countries there is considerable dependence of subordinates on bosses. Subordinates respond by either preferring such dependence (in the form of an autocratic or paternalistic boss), or rejecting it entirely, which in psychology is know as counterdependence: that is dependence, but with a negative sign. Large power distance countries thus show a pattern of polarization between dependence and counterdependence. In these cases, the emotional distance between subordinates and their bosses is large: subordinates are unlikely to approach and contradict their bosses directly."[32]

As we will see later on in this book, the Japanese themselves would not call the relationship between superiors and subordinates 'emotionally distant'. In fact, quite the opposite is the case. However, in Japanese understanding, emotional closeness does not necessarily contain the right – or the wish – to contradict or criticize directly (see chapter 2.1.3.3).

From an early age, children in large power distance are expected to be respectful and obedient towards parents, adults in general and older brothers and sisters. No particular emphasis is placed on independence or self-

---

[32] Hofstede (2003), pp. 27-28

sufficiency in their education. Rather, they receive considerable warmth and care from their parents and elders, creating not only dependence on seniors, but also the need for such dependent relationships.[33]

This pattern is repeated and continued at school and higher educational institutions, where older students often take the role of a tutor, and teachers and professors are considered as absolute authorities, teaching their personal wisdom rather than some impersonal, independent truth. [34]

At work, superiors take on similar positions as teachers, sometimes with even more authority and privileges. There may be large differences in salary, and intricate reporting and hierarchy structures. [35] "The ideal boss, in the subordinates' eyes, is a benevolent autocrat or 'good father'. After some experiences with 'bad fathers', they may ideologically reject the boss's authority completely, while in practice they will comply."[36]

---

[33] cf. Hofstede (2003), p. 32
[34] cf. Hofstede (2003), p. 34
[35] cf. Hofstede (2003), p. 35
[36] Hofstede (2003), p. 35

2.1.1.2 Individualism and collectivism

In collectivist societies, the interest of the group prevails over the interest of the individual, while it is vice versa in individualist societies.[37] The higher the IDV score, the more individualistic is a culture.

Score rank	Country or region	IDV score
1	USA	91
2	Australia	90
3	Great Britain	89
4/5	Canada	80
4/5	Netherlands	80
7	Italy	76
8	Belgium	75
9	Denmark	74
10/11	Sweden	71
10/11	France	71
12	Ireland (Republic of)	70
13	Norway	69
14	Switzerland	68
15	Germany F.R.	67
17	Finland	63
18	Austria	55
20	Spain	51
22/23	Japan	46
30	Greece	35
33/35	Portugal	27

Table 2: Individualism Index (IDV)
Source: Hofstede (2003), p. 53

Japan scores third-lowest among the countries it is to be compared with in this book. The fact that Japan ranks so high in the individualism table (especially compared to other East Asian countries) may be partially

---

[37] cf. Hofstede (2003), p. 50

explained by the traditional family structure, where only the eldest son (plus his wife and children) stays with his parents while the other children leave, which creates a family somewhere between extended and nuclear.[38] It might also be an expression of a change, if not in values, at least in their implementation, which is brought about by industrialization and urbanization. Last but not least, the cause for the high score might be the sample of the study from which the analysed data were obtained from: all of them were employees of a foreign company (IBM). Many guidebooks for foreign companies doing business in Japan recommend to emphasize how different the working atmosphere and conditions they offer are from typical Japanese companies.[39] It might well be that the typical Japanese employee of IBM Japan is not 100 percent congruent with "the typical Japanese".

However, to determine the reason for the high rank would require further studies, which are not subject of this book.

Still, the Japanese culture is more collectivistic than the majority of Western cultures.

Therefore, in the following, the outstanding characteristics of a collectivist society will be described.

> "When children grow up they learn to think of themselves as part of a 'we' group, a relationship which is not voluntary but given by nature. The 'we' group is distinct from other people in society who belong to 'they' groups, of which there are many. The 'we' group (or ingroup) is the major source of one's identity, and the only secure protection one has against the hardships of life. Therefore one owes lifelong loyalty to one's ingroup, and breaking this loyalty is one of the worst things a person can do. Between the person and the ingroup a dependence relationship develops which is both practical and psychological."[40]

---

[38] cf. Hofstede (2003), p. 57
[39] cf. Kammel/Teichelmann (1994), p. 150
[40] Hofstede (2003), p. 50

As explained in chapter 2.1.1.1, dependence on others is an integral part of socialization and education in high power distance cultures, so power distance and collectivism can in fact reinforce each other.

This interdependence, together with intense and continuous social contact that constitutes the daily life in a collectivist culture, makes harmony with ones environment a crucial value. Direct confrontation, criticism and rejection are to be avoided.[41]

> "In the collectivist family children learn to take their bearings from others when it comes to opinions. 'Personal opinions' do not exist: they are predetermined by the group. If a new issue comes up on which there is no established group opinion, some kind of family conference is necessary before an opinion can be given."[42]

Stating one's own opinion without prior confirmation by the ingroup would include the risk to openly (though not necessary knowingly) take a position differing from the rest of the group. This would mean a loss of face not only for the deviating member, but for the whole group.

"Basically, 'face' describes the proper relationship with one's social environment, which is as essential to a person (and that person's family) as the front part of his/her head. The importance of face is the consequence of living in a society that is very conscious of social contexts."[43] In Japan, this need for group conformity is practiced to the extreme that any kind of behaviour standing out from the norm is considered negative. Attracting attention to the individual self happens at the expense of the group. Adapted and representative conduct is therefore not merely desirable, but imperative.[44]

---

[41] cf. Hofstede (2003), p. 58
[42] Hofstede (2003), p. 59
[43] Hofstede (2003), p. 61
[44] Thomas (2001), pp. 70-71

Generally, deviant behaviour is not, as in individualist societies, followed by a feeling of guilt, but rather induces a sense of shame, often felt by the whole group the transgressor belongs to. While guilt is like an individual's inner voice, shame is connected to the outside world: it is only felt if the breach of rules becomes known to others.[45]

People are strictly separated in members of the own ingroup(s), like family members, colleagues, graduates of the same university, and those who do not belong to one's own groups. In other words, the Japanese society is distinguished in those people one has a more or less formal relationship with (even those one has never met, like other graduates from ones own university), and those with which there is no relationship, and which are therefore not relevant, unless there is a coercive reason to deal with them. Persons one has a relationship with belong to 内 *uchi* (inside), all the others are 外 *soto* (outside).

The word *uchi* is not only used for inside, but also, depending on context, for one's home, school, university, organisation or company.[46]

In business life, while it is considered natural for a person to be mainly motivated by their own interest in an individualistic society, ingroups and their interests play an important role as a motivator in a collectivist culture. An employee will place the needs of the group he belongs to above his own needs. Usually, the company at which he is employed will become his number one ingroup, the relationship between him and his employer similar to a family relationship. The employee takes the role of a child paying respect and loyalty to his parents, the employer that of a parent providing for and taking care of the child.[47]

---

[45] cf. Hofstede (2003), p. 60
[46] cf. Nakane (1985), p. 15
[47] cf. Hofstede (2003), pp. 63-64

In general, businessmen in collectivist societies place more importance on personal relationship, than on single tasks or isolated short-term achievements.[48] This statement, which can be found in many publications on Japan, however, should be handled with care: Japanese enterprises, like enterprises all over the world, are generally profit-oriented, and will not even for the sake of a good relationship act totally unreasonable and against the goal of making profit. Nevertheless, they tend to be more long-term relationship oriented than the average Western enterprise, both towards customers and partners, and towards employees.

> "Poor performance of an employee in this relationship is no reason for dismissal: one does not dismiss one's child. Performance and skills, however, do determine what tasks one assigns to an employee. This pattern of relationships is best known from Japanese organizations. In Japan it applies in a strict sense only to the group of permanent employees which may be less than half of the total work force."[49]

---

[48] cf. Hofstede (2003), p. 64
[49] Hofstede (2003), p. 64

2.1.1.3 Masculinity and femininity

Masculinity and femininity are terms coined by Hofstede to describe certain attributes in a culture which are, in the West, generally attributed as 'typically' male or female. "*Masculinity* pertains to societies in which social gender roles are clearly distinct (i.e. men are supposed to be assertive, tough, and focused on material success whereas women are supposed to be more modest, tender, and concerned with the quality of life); *femininity* pertains to societies in which social gender roles overlap (i.e. both men and women are supposed to be modest, tender, and concerned with the quality of life)."[50]

Score rank	Country or region	MAS Score
1	Japan	95
2	Austria	79
4/5	Italy	70
4/5	Switzerland	70
9/10	Great Britain	66
9/10	Germany FR	66
15	USA	62
16	Australia	61
18/19	Greece	57
22	Belgium	54
24	Canada	52
35/36	France	43
37/38	Spain	42
45	Portugal	31
47	Finland	26
50	Denmark	16
51	Netherlands	14
52	Norway	8
53	Sweden	5

Table 3: Masculinity Index (MAS)
Source: Hofstede (2003), p. 84

---

[50] Hofstede (2003), pp. 82-83

Japan is the number one masculine society among all 53 countries researched. A few European countries score close to it, while others, especially Scandinavian countries, are at the opposite end of the table, with the other Western countries spread widely among the midfield. So, Japan should be more masculine than any other country. However, when reading the catalogue of characteristics attributed to masculine cultures, some of them seem totally foreign to the Japanese society. For example, the "family within a masculine society socializes children towards assertiveness, ambition, and competition; organizations in masculine societies stress results, and want to reward it on the basis of equity, i.e., to everyone according to performance."[51] How does this fit with not standing out and valuing personal relationships over tasks? Obviously, the collectivist dimension, though scoring lower than masculinity, has a stronger weight within and thus a larger impact on Japanese society. There is ambition in Japan, but never to the extent of achieving so high as to embarrass other group members. If one wants to advance within one's group, one has to do it carefully and gradually. Just as it is shameful to break rules of conduct, it is also shameful to break positive norms, e.g. the exceeding the average achievement level of one's group. Competition exists, though not with members of one's own ingroup, but rather between different groups, and it may be fierce and very emotional.

Open assertiveness, however, is mostly extenuated by collectivist values.

Families in masculine societies are often led by a dominant, patriarchal father. Mothers are frequently subservient, providing emotional security and warmth for their children; at the same time they may be quite demanding towards them. Equally, as children learn to be competitive and ambitions,

---

[51] Hofstede (2003), p. 93

girls often come to direct their ambition towards their brothers' and later their husband's and children's achievements.[52]

Achievements play a big role in business life, although not so much in the sense of what one does, but what ingroup one is able to enter. A typical Japanese journalist, for example, will introduce himself as "I'm working for publishing house XYZ", rather than "I'm working as a journalist". The framework in which a person moves and operates is more important than the person's individual attributes.[53]

Thus, great effort and time – and also emotion – is invested in the working life, although with a completely different target than in many other masculine but less collectivistic cultures. The company is, for the working members of a masculine collectivist society, often the most important framework or ingroup.

"In a masculine society the ethos tends more toward 'live in order to work', whereas in a feminine society the work ethos would rather be 'work in order to live'."[54]

---

[52] cf. Hofstede (2003), pp. 87-89
[53] cf. Nakane (1985),p. 14
[54] Hofstede (2003), p. 93

2.1.1.4 Uncertainty avoidance

"Uncertainty avoidance can [...] be defined as *the extent to which the members of a culture feel threatened by uncertain or unknown situations*. This feeling is, among other things, expressed through nervous stress and in a need for predictability: a need for written and unwritten rules."[55]

Score rank	Country or region	UAI score
1	Greece	112
2	Portugal	104
5/6	Belgium	94
7	Japan	92
10/15	France	86
10/15	Spain	86
23	Italy	75
24/25	Austria	70
29	Germany FR	65
31/32	Finland	59
33	Switzerland	58
35	Netherlands	53
37	Australia	51
38	Norway	50
41/42	Canada	48
43	USA	46
47/48	Great Britain	35
47/48	Ireland (Republic of)	35
49/50	Sweden	29
51	Denmark	23

Table 4: Uncertainty Avoidance Index (UAI)
Source: Hofstede (2003), p. 113

Again, Japan ranks higher than most Western cultures, with only three European countries surpassing it in uncertainty avoidance. So, typical

---

[55] Hofstede (2003), p. 113

characteristics of an uncertainty avoiding culture may be unfamiliar to most Western negotiators, and will be described in the following.

> "Uncertainty avoidance should not be confused with risk avoidance: uncertainty is to risk as anxiety is to fear. Fear and risk are both focussed on something specific: an object in the case of fear, an event in the case of risk. Risk is often expressed as a percentage of probability that a particular event may happen. Anxiety and uncertainty are both diffuse feelings. [...] Even more than reducing risk, uncertainty avoidance leads to a reduction of *ambiguity*."[56]

In uncertainty avoiding cultures, one usually finds a high degree of structuring within organizations as well as relationships. Predictability of situations and events is a desirable state.[57] Rules and regulations are the tools of choice for bringing about such predictability. They are not necessary because people in uncertainty avoiding cultures tend to behave badly – rather the opposite seems in fact the case – but because they have an emotional need for a certain order of things, an unambiguous and therefore easy to follow code of conduct and social interaction.[58] These rules do not necessarily have to be effective; observing them is not a value in itself, but only in relation to social context. Their function is mainly to fulfil an emotional need for formal structure.[59]

In combination with other cultural dimensions, uncertainty avoidance can create a varied interpretation of the need for rules and formality: "whereas in strong uncertainty avoidance, individualist countries rules will tend to be explicit and written [...], in strong uncertainty avoidance, collectivist countries rules are often implicit and rooted in tradition [...]. This is very

---

[56] Hofstede (2003), p. 116
[57] cf. Hofstede (2003), p. 116
[58] Hofstede (2003), p. 121
[59] Hofstede (2003), p. 121

clearly the case in Japan, and it represents a bone of contention in the negotiations between Western countries and Japan about the opening of the Japanese markets for Western products. The Japanese rightly argue that there are no formal rules preventing the foreign products from being brought in; but the would-be Western importers find themselves up against the implicit rules of the Japanese distribution system which they do not understand."[60]

Early in their education, children in uncertainty avoiding cultures are taught to distinguish ‚safe' and 'dangerous'. These attributes are employed to classify situations, objects and people, and the classification is usually definite and unchangeable.[61] As unfamiliar situations or persons do not have a predefined category they fall under, there is often a tendency to classify them rather on the 'dangerous' side.

As in private life, business life in uncertainty avoiding cultures is full of rules controlling the relationship between employer and employee, their rights and duties and the work process in general. In high power distance cultures, the authority of a superior can reduce or partially replace the need for rules.[62]

As a matter of fact, there are not many formal regulations (like labour laws, working contracts or detailed contracts between companies) in the Japanese business world. However, in spite of Japan's quite high power distance score, there is an infinite number of informal rules to be adhered to, which are not enforced by the superior, but rather by expectations of the respective group concerned (e.g. customers, colleagues of the same department). Chapter 2.1.3 will illustrate many of them further.

---

[60] Hofstede (2003), p. 128
[61] Hofstede (2003), p. 118
[62] cf. Hofstede (2003), pp. 120-121

2.1.1.5 Long term orientation and time perception

During his analysis of the IBM study data, Hofstede became convinced that the study must have a cultural bias, the questionnaires having been created by Western researchers. Consequently, a new cultural value study was created by a Chinese team (exchanging the Western bias with an Eastern), and carried out in 23 countries. Surprisingly, the researchers found similar cultural dimensions as in the IBM study, although the questions had been entirely different.[63] However, one new dimension was found which was not related to the ones from the IBM study: the researchers called it Confucian dynamism, as it encompasses a lot of values which are part of the teachings of Confucius.[64] Its two different poles can also be called long-term versus short term orientation, as the values at the one extreme of the scale are more future-oriented and dynamic, while those at the other extreme are oriented towards the past and present, and more static. On the long term orientation pole, values like persistence, status-consciousness in relationships, thrift, and having a sense of shame are found; the opposite includes steadiness, protecting one's face, respect for traditions and reciprocation in relationships.[65]

---

[63] cf. Hofstede (2003), pp. 160-164
[64] cf. Hofstede (2003), pp. 164-165
[65] cf. Hofstede (2003), pp. 165-166

Score rank	Country or region	LTO score
4	Japan	80
10	Netherlands	44
12	Sweden	33
14	Germany FR	31
15	Australia	31
17	USA	29
18	Great Britain	25
20	Canada	23

Table 5: Long Term Orientation
Source: Hofstede (2003), p. 166

Japan, together with other Asian countries, takes a top position in the long-term orientation table. All the Western cultures researched in the study are far more short-term oriented. This may be somewhat surprising to the Western reader, as East Asian countries are perceived as much more tradition-oriented and concerned with saving face than Western cultures. It must be kept in mind that the study measures the relative weight attached to the various values. Tradition may be more important to East Asian than to Westerners, but values like thrift or perseverance seem to be even more important to them than tradition.[66]

While in many Western cultures, when trying to interpret situations or resolve problems, people tend to search for an absolute *truth*, for "the right solution", cultures with Confucian values (both long- and short-term oriented) refer to *virtue* when trying to determine the appropriate behaviour

---

[66] cf. Hofstede (2003), p. 168

for any given situation. Confucius, in his teachings, concentrated on practical ethics and not on religious truth.[67]

> "What distinguishes the Western from the Eastern religions is their concern with Truth with a capital 'T'. The Western revelation religions share the assumption that there is an absolute Truth which excludes all other truths and which man can possess. [...] Eastern religions are less concerned about Truth. The assumption that there is one Truth which man can possess is absent in their thinking. Buddhism instead stresses the acquisition of insight by meditation. Thus in the East, people will easily absorb elements of different religions. Most Japanese perform both Buddhist and Shinto rituals, although by standards of Western logic the two religious traditions are mutually exclusive."[68]

The emphasis of virtue in form of a certain code of conduct for specified situations, i.e. rituals, may explain the importance that is placed on form and formality in Japan. This will be further described in chapter 2.1.3.3.

For business life, long term orientation means an attitude very supportive of entrepreneurship. Persistence in pursuing ones targets, thrift and economic thinking, and a preference for structure and organisation are all valuable assets for business activities to be successful.[69] Though these values are found in many Western cultures, especially in highly industrialized countries, they seem to have an even larger importance in Japan.

Less common in the West are the need for harmony in social relationships, and the imperative for having a sense of shame. These two values, in business life, are especially meaningful for maintaining positive relationships with partners and customers, and for keeping one's commitments.[70] While these results are equally desirable in the West, they are at least partially based

---

[67] Hofstede (2003), p. 171
[68] Hofstede (2003), pp. 131-132
[69] cf. Hofstede (2003), p. 168
[70] Hofstede (2003), p. 168

on different values, and may therefore be achieved by totally different measures and behaviours.

When speaking about long-term orientation, time perception in general is an aspect to be considered. Time perception is not entirely linked to the cultural dimension of long-/short-term orientation. It also relates to individualism and collectivism: "In more individualist societies like the USA, the system's stress is more on short-term results than in more collectivist societies like Japan or even Germany, as in an individualist environment the responsible people may change employers at short notice."[71]
According to E.T. Hall and M. Hall-Reed, cultures can be divided in monochronic and polychronic time perceptions. Monochronic cultures are clock-oriented, tend to think and act structured, precise and systematic, whereas people with a polychronic attitude are event-oriented, and tend to think more holistic and less structured.[72] While most Western countries are strongly or moderately monochronic, South and Southeast Asia belong to the cultures with a polychronic attitude.[73] In Japan, this attitude mainly shows in the emphasis of personal relationships and their long-term maintenance.

The term "long-term" itself is obviously interpreted very differently in different cultures: "If American and Japanese employ during negotiation the sentence "we need to establish a long-term cooperation", they have surely a completely different time conception. Americans mean perhaps five years, Japanese mean 20 years."[74]

The previous chapters have explained the four plus one dimensions of culture in a very basic way (and already with a bias towards describing

---

[71] Hofstede (2003), p. 155
[72] cf. Gaspardo (2000), p. 49
[73] cf. Gaspardo (2000), p. 52
[74] Gaspardo (2000), p. 49

specifically Japanese aspects). Outstanding and typical characteristics of the Japanese culture will be the subject of the following chapters.

2.1.2 Language, communication and information exchange

What probably stands out most when trying to communicate with citizens of a foreign country is the first hurdle one encounters: the language. And few languages could be more alien to the Westerner than Japanese. Yet, it is by no means all that there is to communication. The following chapters will focus on the various aspects of communication characteristic for Japan.

2.1.2.1 Language

The Japanese language is not in any way related to any Western language. There are similarities to Korean, and suspected early influences from Altaic and Malayo-Polynesian languages. In the 6th century AD, the Chinese writing system was adopted by Japanese scholars. So today's written Japanese consists of originally Chinese characters and two sets of syllable alphabets derived from them.[75] Otherwise there are no resemblances, not to speak of genetic relationships, to any other language. Both unfamiliarity and writing system make the Japanese language all but easy to learn for foreigners.

But language is more than a communication tool (or in case of foreigners a hurdle): it represents essentially the way members of a culture think, or rather express their thoughts to themselves. "Words are obstinate vehicles: our thinking is affected by the categories for which words are available in our

---

[75] cf. Kodansha (1994), p. 292

language."[76] So by looking at characteristics of a language, one can learn a lot about the mindset of the people who speak it.

Japanese has a much wider range of politeness than most Western languages. There are five different levels in which one can address superiors, equals and subordinates, including different grammatical forms, vocabulary and syntax. By leaving out or adding words, changing word endings or using different personal pronouns, a speaker immediately makes clear his hierarchical position in relation to the listener. Like anything related to communication in Japan, polite language is highly context sensitive. Depending on how close conversation partners are, politeness can be anything from appropriate (e.g. if a vendor speaks to his customer in a very humble way) to insulting (e.g. if a student applies extremely polite language to a close friend, implying rejection). Without a context, it is difficult for the Japanese to find the proper way of speaking to a person. Thus, a total stranger with no social contact or obvious hierarchical position may not always be met with the typical Japanese politeness he expects:

> "If two people are strangers, the communication is apt to be abrupt and rude. Once two Japanese people know each other by name, they become much more polite, with expectations of politeness from the other party. As the relationship between people becomes closer, they become more like allies in working for their mutual good. Over time, if their relationship becomes more intimate, they may drop all barriers and actually achieve a status of informal intimate trust, without posturing."[77]

This central role of context within communication is not only restricted to hierarchy. The Japanese, as an insular race, are a relatively homogeneous people with about 1500 years of (recorded) common history. This shared

---

[76] Hofstede (2003), p. 213
[77] Wichert (2004), p. 1

background reduces the necessity to say things explicitly; with very few words, much more meaning is transferred than in many Western (i.e. low-context) communications.[78] The Japanese (i.e. high-context) listener detects a lot of the information the speaker actually wants to convey in the environment, the situation or the person speaking without the speaker ever vocalizing it.[79]

This puts a high degree of responsibility for the success of communication on the listener, as he must 'listen with all senses' to detect possible hidden meanings behind the words actually spoken.[80] In case of communicating with foreigners, it makes it not only difficult for foreigners to understand the message that is supposed to be conveyed, but also sometimes leads the Japanese to mis- or overinterpret the messages the foreigner is trying to send (see case study 9). In case the Japanese communication partner is aware of the lack of shared background, he may react by trying to balance it and requesting infinite amounts of contextual information.

> "This can be exasperating for business counterparts who feel that they have provided enough information already. Rather than focusing only on a potential partner's business proposal or the specific task at hand, a Japanese may take a more holistic approach and want to know about the partner's character and history; they will be reluctant to pursue a joint task until a relationship has been established."[81]

For a culture scoring rather high in uncertainty avoidance, this interpretation-intensive way of communicating may seem to include quite a lot of ambiguity. Here again another dimension seems to prevail over uncertainty avoidance. The collectivistic attitude makes indirect speech an essential way of avoiding to insult the conversation partner or audience. "The Japanese

---

[78] cf. Gundling (1999), pp. 8-9
[79] cf. Hofstede (2003), p. 60
[80] cf. Gaspardo (2000), pp. 30-31
[81] Gundling (1999), p. 9

desire to maintain relationships by avoiding confrontation often leads them to give ambiguous responses which are misinterpreted by foreigners, causing misunderstandings and sometimes bad feelings. In a culture like the U.S., which values directness, it is a virtue to "Say what you mean, and mean what you say." In Japan, doing this often causes undesirable results for oneself and the organization."[82]

One striking example of avoiding directness in communication is the Japanese use of the words "yes" and "no". Plainly translated as はい *hai* and いいえ *iie*, these very basic words are employed in a totally different way than in the West.
""Yes" in Japan can mean anything from "I'm listening to you," to "I understand what you're saying" to "I understand what you're saying, but don't agree with you.""[83] G. Thomas suggests that the English word "roger" might be a more appropriate translation for the Japanese *hai*.[84]
Iie, on the other hand, is rarely ever used. The Japanese language has various expressions to help avoid saying no directly, like 違います *chigaimasu* ("this is not correct"), 難しいでしょう *muzukashii deshō* ("it could be difficult"), 厳しい *kibishii* ("it is hard to do", implying that it is unkind to insist on such a thing), or 今回はちょっと *konkai wa chotto* ("a little this time", having the connotation of "please give in to me a little this time", suggesting the possibility that next time a request is made, it will be approved). Of course, these expressions all express negation, and have the same consequences as a direct no would in a Western culture. But by wording it implicitly, the rejection or denial is softened and easier to take in and accept for the other party. This is practiced even in situations where a no has no negative implication at all.

---

[82] Gundling (1999), p. 22
[83] Gundling (1999), p. 22
[84] cf. Thomas (2001), p. 173

Considering the subtleties and pitfalls of the Japanese language, the question arises if a foreigner intending to negotiate with Japanese people should actually learn to speak it? There seems to be a great deal of disagreement among experts on this topic.

There are those who claim that only by understanding how people express themselves in their native tongue one can understand what they say in his own language.[85] Especially for a language which is not related to one's own, this is true to some extent. Also, speaking the language is a considerable facilitator for achieving integration into a culture, if the foreigner is actually living in Japan.[86] In the case of companies trying to establish themselves on the Japanese market, the network of relationships necessary to enable success there, communicating in Japanese seems to be not only a matter of being a polite guest, but imperative for survival.[87]

Besides direct communication, there is the issue of information gathering. Japan is a country with a vast abundance of published and printed information on political, economical and technical backgrounds, but of course, the majority of publications is in the native language of the supposed audience. To those understanding Japanese, Japan is in fact a "country without secrets".[88]

On the other hand, foreigners do not automatically ascend to being integrated in the Japanese culture by speaking Japanese.[89] While a foreigner with very basic language skills will usually be met with considerable

---

[85] cf. Rowland (1994), p. 49
[86] cf. Kammel/Teichelmann (1994), p. 76
[87] cf. Großmann (1992), p. 250
[88] cf. Großmann (1992), p. 250
[89] cf. Thomas (2001), p. 49

enthusiasm on the Japanese side, and thus gain a sympathy bonus, a businessman with just enough skills to negotiate in Japanese may find himself at a disadvantage, as he may not always be able to or get across his point, or fully grasp what his negotiation partner is saying. In fact, the author has met Western expatriate managers in Japan who explicitly follow a strategy of not learning to speak Japanese, forcing their negotiation partners to either speak English or not do business with them.

The most common argument for not learning Japanese is that all the Japanese speak English anyway. English is taught at almost every school in Japan as a second language. A written test of English is part of the access exam necessary for attending university.[90]
However, English language education focuses on reading and writing skills and grammatical rules, neglecting speaking practice and listening comprehension.[91] This circumstance can make it hard for the foreigner (whose native tongue may not be English either) to understand a Japanese person speaking English. Moreover, it makes the Japanese very self-conscious and reluctant to speak English even if they have good language skills. As form and beauty is valued very highly in Japan, to the extent that it sometimes prevails over contents and meaning (as will be described in chapter 2.1.3.3), and as making a mistake in public is considered extremely embarrassing (see chapter 2.1.1.2), fear of speaking incorrect English may actually keep a person from speaking, even if they have something important to say.

So the answer to the question if foreigners should learn Japanese, one is tempted to say in typical Japanese manner, is yes and no. Basic language

---

[90] cf. Kodansha International (1994), p. 176
[91] cf. Gundling (1999), p. 29

skills are recommendable for anyone going to Japan for more than touristic reasons. But particularly for businesspeople, instead of going through the trouble of learning the complex and unfamiliar language, it may be more advisable to employ someone fluent in Japanese and their native language or English, and who is not tied by group loyalty to the negotiation partner.

2.1.2.2 Paraverbal and non-verbal communication

Paraverbal communication refers to additional means of transferring messages that are applied to the actual words spoken, such as intonation, tone of voice or pauses between speaking. Non-verbal communication encompasses all other means of expression, like gestures, facial expressions, posture etc.

> "People from high context cultures such as Japan will sometimes choose implicit, nonverbal communication over explicit, verbal communication. They may feel that verbal communication is too blunt or unnecessarily obvious, whereas expressing yourself nonverbally is more subtle and considerate."[92]

Generally, the Japanese language does not feature a very expressive intonation. Also, there are not supposed to be breaks between the words of a sentence, neither in writing nor speaking. It's almost impossible to tell a question from a declarative sentence, or a technical lecture from the recital of a poem, just by listening to the intonation. Unfortunately (though understandably), many Japanese apply this way of speaking to the English language too, which makes them hard to understand for a foreigner in both tongues.

---

[92] Gundling (1999), p. 30

The Japanese are known for the long periods of silence that their conversations are punctuated with. This often makes the Western communication partner uncomfortable, and they feel compelled to fill these silences with more information or questions. This, on the other hand tends to irritate the Japanese, who feel untimely interrupted in their communication process.[93] Silence, from a Japanese perspective, can contain all kinds of messages, ranging from "I'm thinking about what you said and trying to understand it" through "I'm comfortable in your presence, therefore speaking is not required." to "I disagree, but don't want to say it. Please make another suggestion."[94]

One other means of communicating without words very frequently applied is laughter. Just like silence, it can express a wide variety of meanings.

> "The Japanese have an expression for one type of laughter, "Aisō-warai," which can be translated as "polite laughter," "diplomatic laughter" or even "fake laughter." One meaning of the polite laugh is that the person does not understand the English being spoken. Therefore the laugh may indicate confusion or embarrassment, and even a hope that the speaker will clarify. Another meaning of the "polite laugh" is the reluctance of the Japanese to give a direct negative response to what the speaker said. In other words, instead of saying a direct "No" or "I disagree," the Japanese gives a polite laugh to send that message to the speaker."[95]

Other things to bear in mind when communicating with the Japanese are their preferences regarding personal distance, touching behaviour, eye contact, and gestures.[96] For all these points except personal distance, the general rule "the less the better" can be applied. The Japanese, though overpopulated cities and crowded restaurants and trains may suggest

---

[93] Gaspardo (2000), p. 38
[94] cf. Gundling (1999), p. 31
[95] Gundling (1999), p. 30
[96] cf. Gaspardo (2000), pp. 39-44

otherwise, greatly value personal space and do not like to be touched by people they are not closely related or friends with.

Eye contact, if it lasts longer than one or two seconds, is considered aggressive and provoking.[97] The Western negotiator trying to signal honesty and establish good relationships by intensive eye contact may create a very uncomfortable atmosphere.

Just like intonation, gestures and facial expressions are subtle to non-existent in Japanese conversations. This is partially related to the concept of *tatemae*, of keeping a harmonious appearance no matter what is going on inside. (*Tatemae* will be explained in detail in chapter 2.1.3.3)

2.1.2.3 Information flow

"Each culture has its own information flow. It is important to know that in some cultures – such as the Italian, Spanish, Latin American and in the Arab World – information spreads rapidly and moves almost as if it had a life of its own. [...] How information flows in a culture is the single most important thing for the outsider to learn, since cultural differences in information flow are often the greatest stumbling block to international understanding."[98]

In Japan, it seems, information travels at the speed of light at least. Informal communication channels are abundant and used extensively.

"In high information context communications the information channels are seldom overloaded because people are in constant contact with each other. They are continuously – superficially – informed about everything, because they always talk with each other about everything. In high-flow information cultures, being out of touch is to cease to exist."[99]

---

[97] cf. Gaspardo (2000), p. 44
[98] Gaspardo (2000), p. 42
[99] Gaspardo (2000), p. 42

Information, for an uncertainty avoiding culture, is crucial to reduce ambiguity and insecurity.[100] Every bit of information might prove important in any future situation; decision making based on thoroughly researched facts, even if they are not directly connected to the decision, seems much safer than risking a potential danger or error by overlooking something.

In business, competitors are meticulously researched, and no matter how hard they try to keep theirs secrets, every market participant is well informed about all the others in his field of activity.[101]

> "Businesspeople from low context, task-oriented cultures tend to limit their focus to "need to know" information, which means information that *they think* they or another person needs to know to complete the task at hand. They don't want to be inundated with "nice to know" information -- there isn't time to deal with it all. However, in a high-context, holistic culture such as Japan, "nice to know" *is* "need to know.""[102]

Thus the foreign visitor may be overwhelmed, both by the abundance of information he is expected to take in, and by the extensive information his Japanese negotiation partners request from him.

> "Foreigners from low context cultures such as Germany or the U.S. often find Japanese explanations or presentations confusing. Rather than hearing a concise statement of key points supported by facts and examples, they may find themselves lost in a spiral of background information, with no explicitly expressed conclusion. In trying to communicate the whole context, Japanese often lead up to the point through a gradual accumulation of background details. When enough background has been given, it may even be felt redundant to verbalize the conclusion, as it should be obvious by that time."[103]

---

[100] cf. Gaspardo (2000), p. 58
[101] Nakane (1985), p. 126
[102] Gundling (1999), p. 14
[103] Gundling (1999), pp. 14-15

This leaves the Western listener at a loss, as he will consider the conclusion as the most important part of the communication message.

Providing information, especially at the often vague requests from the Japanese, is often a tedious process of giving the requested data, then receiving another, more detailed request, answering that with more data, only to be confronted with more questions on the same subject. At the same time, foreign businesspeople can encounter considerable difficulty in obtaining information themselves in Japan. Not belonging to any ingroups, and thus cut off from the informal information network, it may be hard at the beginning to acquire anything but very superficial facts and data. It takes time and a lot of networking to gain access to the vital communication channels.[104]

2.1.3 Working ethics and ideals
2.1.3.1 Education and career in Japan

For better being able to understand Japanese values related to business, a brief description of typical elements and principles of education and working life in Japan will follow below.

The Japanese school system consists of elementary school (6 years), junior high school (3 years, both compulsory) and high school (3 years, voluntary). Public schools are free of charge, but private schools have by far the better reputation and are thus more popular, even though they can be extremely expensive.[105] The choice of high school (and to some extent even middle school) is often based on the number of graduates being accepted to

---

[104] cf. Gundling (1999), p. 15
[105] cf. Thomas (2001), p. 187

reputable universities.[106] At an early age, Japanese children get accustomed to elite selection and pressure to perform, as the university one attends has great influence on what kind of career one can aspire to. In addition to school, they are often sent to so-called 塾 *juku*, coaching schools for private lessons.

The university entrance examination is even more important than high school graduation; many students take a year off (i.e. attend special preparation schools) after high school to be able to prepare for it sufficiently. Who wants to attend the most renowned universities has to go to extremes: there is a saying that who sleeps for four hours a night will pass the test, and who sleeps five hours will fail.[107] The term "examination hell" (試験地獄 *shiken jigoku*) is often used for this time of life.

Still, 97% of students graduate from high-school, and over 44% go to college or university.[108] Parents are willing to spend considerable amounts of money for tuition fees, to the extent of raising credits and closing special education savings contracts at the birth of their children.[109]

This investment is expected to pay off after students graduate. If they have attended a renowned university, they can be almost certain to be recruited by a large company. The subject they have actually studied often plays a secondary role, especially for administrative (i.e. non-technical) positions.

Most larger companies hire a new class of graduates each year, and through extensive training on the job are able to build up their own management staff without ever recruiting personnel from other companies in mid-career. Usually each company has their preferred institution(s) to recruit from, and

---

[106] cf. Pohl (1992), p. 243
[107] cf. Pohl (1992), p. 244
[108] cf. MPHPT (2003), p. 191
[109] cf. Pohl (1992), p. 244-248

with each class of graduates they employ the ties to the respective university grow stronger.[110]

> "As mentioned above, university recruiting is still by far the most popular method for large Japanese companies to hire new professionals, and there is a great deal of prestige that accompanies being hired by a major Japanese firm. As a result, university recruiting is extremely competitive among companies that are especially intent on hiring graduates with engineering and other technical degrees."[111]

Once hired by a large traditional company, the new employee is not likely to leave it again before reaching retirement age. Although this is not formally written out in contracts, lifetime employment is still common practice in Japan.[112]

Traditionally, if an employees performance is not satisfactory, instead of being laid off, he is transferred to a position that is less demanding, often at an affiliate company or subcontractor. This may include lower salary, but is still considered better than loosing one's job entirely.[113]

Changing jobs in mid-career, even on one's own initiative, is regarded as negative, and is generally only done when significant problems occur. Recently, this principle seems to be softening somewhat, due to economic stagnation and international competition, but Japan is still far away from "hire-and-fire" or the Western ideal of regularly changing jobs for the sake of one's own career advancement.[114]

The loyalty to one's employer is considerably larger than in the West. The company is not just the place where one earns one's living, but serves as

---

[110] cf. Gross (1998), p. 14
[111] Gross (1998), p. 14
[112] cf. Gross (1998), p. 3
[113] Gross (1998), p. 5
[114] cf. Gross (1998), p. 15

one's primary ingroup,[115] and thus to a large part as the source of one's identity. The relationship between employer and employee is not merely contractual and an exchange of performance for payment, but an emotional one. The employee is supposed to be highly loyal to the company and invest most of his energy into the company's success. The employer in turn has an obligation to take care of the employee's well-being, which even extends to his private life.[116] Accordingly, the company's advancement is much more important to Japanese employees from all hierarchy levels in their day-to-day work than to the average employee in the West, where the company's long-term fate is rather left to top level management.[117] The bond with the organisation prevails over bonds to a group of specific job functions or a hierarchy level, creating a strong corporate identity and unconditional loyalty to one's employer.[118]

Still, hierarchy levels do play an important role within the individual's career. Being promoted, however, is not so much based on one's performance, as on seniority, i.e. the duration one has been employed with the company. Performance and skills are criteria, but they alone do not usually justify a promotion to a higher level within the company. "In most cases in which a younger person of unusual ability is "promoted" over the heads of more senior employees, employers often refrain from increasing the individual's title or salary until he or she has gained more seniority and age."[119]
Advancement happens at a slow pace: according to a study inquiring 100 Japanese employees holding a university degree who worked for a large corporation, it takes an average of nine years after entering the company to

---

[115] cf. Sakamoto (1976), pp. 117-118
[116] cf. Nakane (1985), p. 15
[117] cf. Sakamoto (1976), p. 137
[118] cf. Kammel/Teichelmann (1994), p. 143
[119] Gross (1998), p. 2

reach the level of chief clerk (係長 *kakarichō*). After 16 (i.e. another 7) years, one can attain the position of section manager (課長 *kachō*). About 30% of the questioned employees were promoted to department head (部長 *buchō*), at an average of 24 years after entering the company.[120] Thus, a major career move happens every 8 years on average. Especially during the time before being promoted to chief clerk, the employee is assigned a new position about every three to five years, to give him a broad overview of all fields of operation within the company, and to expand his skills and knowledge.[121] Through this system, the employee obtains a broad range of skills rather than specialized knowledge.

Therefore, the Western negotiator should not automatically assume a shared professional background which is a hundred percent congruent with his own, even if his counterpart holds the same position and job title as himself.

> "The Japanese corporate hierarchy, along with a strong tradition of group consensus, has had a significant impact on the skills that employees acquire. For example, mid-career managers (who are usually between the ages of 40 and 50) are typically only allowed to make decisions on routine matters, and often make these decisions as part of a large group. Mid-level managers also act as mediators between their subordinates and superiors. As a result, 40-year-old Japanese managers do not have as much decision-making experience as Western managers of similar age, and will often be uncomfortable making important decisions (especially in the course of negotiations) without the approval of their superiors."[122]

Like the principle of lifetime employment, the seniority system seems to be slowly giving way to a more performance-oriented promotion scheme due to increased international competition.[123] Job rotation and the ideal of

---

[120] cf. Abe (1995), pp. 31-33
[121] cf. Gross (1998), p. 3
[122] Gross (1998), p. 2
[123] cf. Gross (1998), p. 3

generalists with a broad view rather than specialists however seem to remain unchanged in Japan.

The ideal of a broad view is also reflected in the salary system: Usually, employees receive a fixed salary, plus an annual bonus, which is closely linked to the whole company's success rather than to his own performance, or the results achieved by his department or team. So, while the employee can contribute to the payment and the height of his bonus, he is highly dependent on all his colleagues' performance, which further strengthens his ties with the company.

Tariff working hours of Japanese employees are not extremely higher than in many European countries. Still, the actual number of hours worked is about 20% higher than e.g. in Germany, mainly due to overtime and fewer days of leave. According to Japanese labour law, an employee is entitled to a minimum of 15 days of holiday; however, less than 50% of all employees actually take all of these days off.[124] Taking holidays is felt to happen at one's colleagues' expenses.[125]

The following chart shows a comparison of working hours in manufacturing in Japan with various Western countries:

---

[124] cf. Thomas (2001), pp. 224-225
[125] cf. Thomas (2001), p. 67

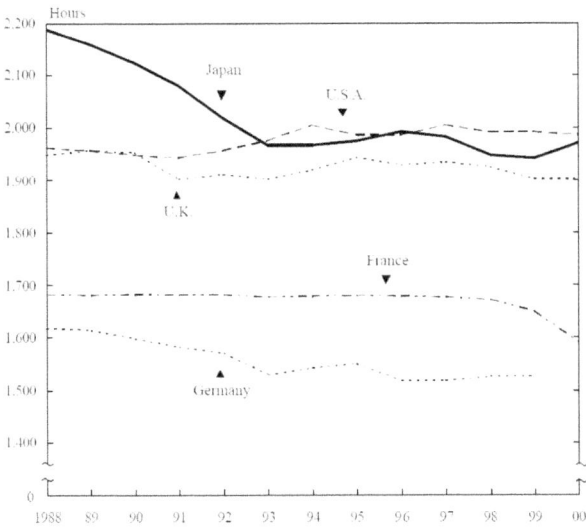

Figure 1: Total hours worked per annum by country (manufacturing)
Source: MPHPT (2003), p. 153

A clear downward trend since 1988 (when there was a revision in Labour Law) is discernible, reducing the gap between Japan and the West considerably (although there are obviously substantial gaps between various Western countries as well).

What the statistics do not show are the many hours a Japanese employee spends with his colleagues after office hours, for socializing and discussing business informally. These meetings are not officially compulsory. Yet they are not only indispensable for career advancement, they are a necessary means of integration into the group one is working with. Considering the perspective of lifetime employment, and the general collectivistic attitude, there is little possibility to avoid or decline those meetings.[126] In addition to strengthening ties and good relationships between employees through common recreational activities, informal after hours meetings are the one

---

[126] cf. Thomas (2001), p. 244

opportunity to speak one's mind freely. Especially after a certain amount of alcohol is consumed, criticism of superiors' or colleagues' actions is acceptable and not met with any sanctions. Problems which are not discussed in the office can be addressed openly, and superiors, who cannot tolerate any challenge of their leadership and decisions in the rigidly hierarchical office environment can use the pretext of the critic being drunk to grant him freedom of speech and obtain his subordinates' honest assessment of what has happened during the day. Though these drunk evening discussions are never mentioned in the formal environment at the office, the information and opinions gathered there are often included in the management's decision making.[127]

2.1.3.2 Leadership and motivation

In a society as hierarchy-oriented and collectivistic as Japan, it is not hard to imagine that there are major differences in management style to the individualistic and often more egalitarian West. However, Japanese management does not function as strictly top-down as one might expect. A group leader, department head or CEO, while he is treated with great respect and formality, is not so much an absolute monarch as he is a provident father. The employees' high degree of loyalty towards the company is "rewarded" with an all-encompassing care and providence for them from the management side. This extends not only to all issues at the workplace, but also to the employees' private lives.[128]

The leader's authority is based on his position within the group rather than on his skills and achievements. The most important factor of leadership is the emotional bond between superior and subordinates, which is established

---

[127] cf. Thomas (2001), pp. 244-245
[128] cf. Kammel/Teichelmann (1994), p. 143

informally.[129] The leader is supposed to place great value on these emotional ties, and to keep them active and intact at all times.

A good superior practices *onjōshugi* (温情主義, paternalism, showing a warm heart), meaning that he generally displays a benevolent attitude towards his subordinates, does not criticise or discipline them and is ready to forgive mistakes.[130]

Usually it is not a necessary requirement that the leader of a group be extraordinarily skilled or brilliant to justify his authority. In fact, subordinates are happy to compensate for any weakness their superior may have, changing the unilateral dependence into a system of mutual interdependency. [131] Insofar, Hofstede's finding that there is more interdependence between superior and subordinate in small power distance cultures, and more unilateral dependence of the subordinate on his superior in large power distance cultures[132], is not a hundred percent valid for Japan. On the other hand, this may precisely be the reason why a culture so hierarchy-focused as Japan does not score top in the power distance ranking.

The social principle on which these dependency relationships are based is known as *on* (恩, favour, obligation) and *giri* (義理, duty, sense of duty) in Japanese. If one receives a favour or favourable treatment (i.e. *on*) from someone who is not in any way obliged to this behaviour, one has the duty to return this favour with an equivalent one. As the exact value of immaterial favours is impossible to determine, such favours can never be completely returned. The *on*-receiver is obliged to the *on*-giver indefinitely, and automatically assumes a lower hierarchical position relative to his

---

[129] cf. Nakane (1985), pp. 92-93
[130] cf. Sakamoto (1976), p. 144
[131] Nakane (1985), p. 95
[132] cf. Hofstede (2003), pp. 27-28

benefactor.[133] A relationship which is based on this mechanism can not easily be terminated; the *on*-receiver is bound to the *on*-giver if he likes it or not.[134] *Giri*, on the other hand, is a general concept of social obligation, referring to "how things ought to be done". It encompasses all social norms and rules that have to be complied with regardless of one's own feelings.[135] While an *on*-relationship is always hierarchical, *giri* obliges peers as well as superiors and subordinates.[136]

These two motivators which make Japanese subordinates follow their leader often unconditionally and display conform behaviour rather than independency, is sometimes hard to comprehend for individualistic Westerners. It seems an all-too materialistic calculation of value and counter-value. However, the principle of *on* and *giri* is one of the most powerful motivators not only at the workplace but throughout the Japanese's whole social life. Visitors to Japan should be well aware of it, as they automatically enter an *on*- or *giri*-relationship as soon as they receive support in coping with their new environment from a Japanese person. And for negotiations, the principle of obligation and counter-obligation can be used as a powerful tool if the negotiator is aware of its mechanism and implications.

2.1.3.3 Hierarchy and formality

In chapter 2.1.1.1 the importance of hierarchical relationships in Japan has already been described. As most other areas of life, the business world is pervaded by power distance, be it the hierarchical relationship among organisation members, the ranking of companies within their field of industry, the different levels of prestige attached to universities, or the near

---

[133] cf. Befu (1985), pp. 166-168
[134] cf. Thomas (2001), p. 128
[135] cf. Befu (1985), pp. 169-170
[136] cf. Hamabata (1986), p. 362

ownership-relation [137] that exists between vendor and customers. This is displayed in countless patterns of behaviour, informal rules of conduct and ways of speaking and communicating:

> "Seating arrangements are based on hierarchy. In a taxi, the seat behind the driver is for the highest ranking person while the seat next to the driver is for the lowest ranking person. Order of speaking is also hierarchical, in that often the highest ranking person speaks last. Japanese language itself reflects hierarchy. A person of higher status speaks polite or casual speech, whereas the person of lower status uses "super-polite" or "respectful" speech (*keigo*)." [138]

When negotiations take place between two companies, it is expected that each side sends negotiators of the same age and hierarchical rank, so that each attendee has an appropriate communication partner.[139] Job titles are of central importance, to the extent that some employees possess different business cards with different job titles for different negotiation partners. However, these titles do not necessarily reflect the actual hierarchical position of an employee. Informal group structures often differ from formal and visible organisation. It can be devastating for a group leader if his formal position does not correspond to informal structures of leadership. If his subordinates are in an obligation relationship with another (informal) leader, they will be loyal to him only towards the outside world. Behind the scenes they will not comply with his directives and carry out his decisions.[140]
Therefore it is not easy for the outsider to discern who is responsible for what within a group. Still, formal positions are of immense significance to the impression the group creates towards non-members as they reflect the order and operating mode of the whole Japanese social system. A subordinate can

---

[137] cf. Gundling (1999), p. 16
[138] Gundling (1999), p. 7
[139] cf. Gundling (1999), p. 6
[140] cf. Nakane (1985), pp. 92-93

be much more influential or skilled than his superior, but in the presence of outsiders he must never show anything but the greatest respect towards his leader, who will otherwise suffer a loss of face.[141]

This loss of face would be embarrassing not only to the group leader, but also to the employee who caused it and to those who witnessed it. *Kata* (形), the proper form of things, plays a central role in human interaction, and is to be preserved in any situation.

To maintain the proper form, it is important to keep up *tatemae* (建前, the face one shows to the outside world) and to hide one's true feelings if they are likely to disturb the harmony (本音, *honne*). In principle, this concept is not unique to Japan: in the West, too, what one says often differs from what one thinks. But while this is considered untruthful and negative in the West, it is a sign of bad education and extreme impoliteness to speak one's mind freely without considering the effect on the listener's feeling of harmony, thus endangering the smooth functioning of social life.[142] There are occasions on which the Japanese show their *honne*, but these are kept to the private environment, where one can be sure not to hurt the reputation of one's family, company or nation.[143]

While many members of Western cultures feel that their inner reality, their *honne*, defines who they are, and cannot be easily changed, in Japan, the question "Who am I?" is directly dependent on the question "Who is my audience?". There are various different words for "I" in the Japanese language, which are used according to context and conversation partner.[144] A study carried out among visiting Japanese students at an American university showed that they gave different answers to the same questions

---

[141] cf. Nakane (1985), p. 98
[142] cf. Hamabata (1986), pp. 357-358
[143] cf. Thomas (2001), p. 126
[144] cf. Thomas (2001), pp. 145-146

depending on where and how they had been questioned. Also, the opinions of most students were remarkably uniform although they did not have the opportunity to consult with each other before or during the enquiry. It turned out that depending on the situational context of the enquiry, the students had tried to give answers they thought were expected of them, in their role as either member of a group of visiting students, or private person.[145]

This context-related Japanese self will often make it hard for a foreigner to determine the true meaning of what is actually spoken in an official context. It takes a lot of sensitiveness and experience, as well as sufficient information on context and circumstances, to tell *tatemae* from *honne*. Failure may lead to frustration and to developing the prejudice that all Japanese are lying and dishonest, which can be extremely harmful to the negotiation process. To avoid this happening, the Western negotiator must keep in mind that the instrument of *tatemae* is not meant to cause harm to others. Keeping a harmonious outside appearance is vital to a collectivist society to function, and also helps to avoid uncertainty: "When all members of society understand and conform to the *kata*, ambiguity is removed. This shared understanding breaks down when Japanese interact across cultures."[146]

Luckily, in many cases, the Japanese do not expect foreigners to be proficient in the more formal displays of *kata* (like bowing or handing over business cards), and thus will forgive superficial errors readily. The one mistake one should not make, however, is urging a Japanese to give up his principle of keeping up *tatemae*. Asking for a statement of personal opinion, especially in public situations, can cause great embarrassment and discomfort, and will often result in permanently damage to the personal relationship.[147]

---

[145] cf. Thomas (2001), p. 125
[146] Gundling (1999), p. 7
[147] cf. Thomas (2001), p. 128

The Japanese themselves, if they want to find out about someone's private opinion, will wait for a private occasion (e.g. when going out together, or when there is no audience), or try to discreetly interview people close to the person whose opinion they are interested in. This is one more reasons why shared recreational activities after hours are so important and frequent among Japanese employees.

So it is advisable for the foreigner to try and establish a close personal relationship with at least one Japanese group member, through common private activities or intense co-operation (or maybe by granting him a favour which one is not obliged to), who can then function as an interpreter of the statements of the other group members.

2.1.3.4 Decision making and responsibility

One very ceremonial procedure in Japanese business life is the formal decision making process known as *ringi seido* (稟議制度).

> "The *ringi* system consists of a written proposal which is circulated among all the people who will be affected by the decision. It is circulated by a predetermined route based on hierarchy, starting lower in the organization and working its way up. When the *ringi* proposal reaches each person's desk, they read it, sometimes make a few minor adjustments or suggestions, and then put their personal seal on it (in place of a signature in the West). By the time the *ringi* document has "made the rounds" and received everyone's seal, all the people involved in the decision have had a chance to give input and are in agreement on the decision. [...]The end result is that the responsibility is spread out among many individuals and not left with one or only a few. This has the advantage of more people feeling

responsibility and "owning" the decision; the drawback is that sometimes no one really is accountable for the decision or the results."[148]

The second large disadvantage is of course that this procedure of decision-making, at least at first glance, takes a considerable amount of time. However, involving everyone concerned in a decision at an early stage can actually save time in the implementation:

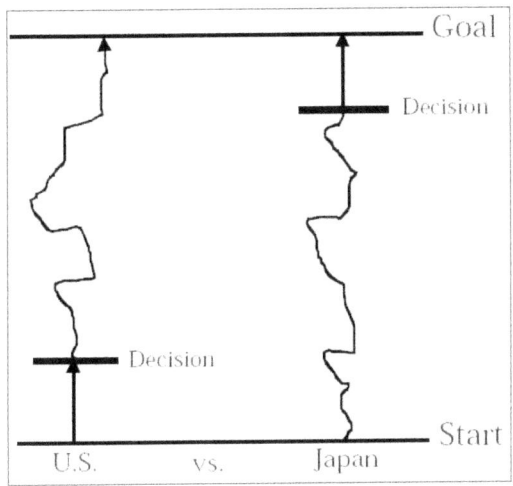

Figure 2: Decision making and implementation in the US and Japan
Source: Gundling (1999), p. 11

Even if there is no formal procedure with a written document, a similar process is often carried out informally.

At first glance, this may seem a highly democratic way of making decisions by group consensus. However, the process is not designed to give everyone the opportunity to state his personal opinion, but to allow each group member to get in line with the feelings of the other group members and to adapt one's opinion before one has to state it officially.

---

[148] Gundling (1999), p. 10

"This is clearly a form of persuasion, but takes the form of self directed persuasion, to match the beliefs of the individual to those of the group. The "rhetoric" in such a situation is merely the informative description of the views of the group. The real persuasion is done by the listener, in response to the hierarchical nature of the group, and the inclination to keep peaceful relations with others".[149]

On less official occasions, opinions can be stated more directly. Frequently after hours meetings are used to communicate problems in the decision making process, or to make concessions which were impossible in an official context. At these meetings taking place in restaurants or bars, negotiations often proceed at a much faster pace than during the daytime at the office. However, decisions already taken during official daytime meetings will not be revised at these 'after-parties', as this would result in a loss of face. The main purpose of after hours meetings is to improve personal relationships and strengthen existing ties. Decisions taken can be discussed and questioned, but the resulting compromises or changes will only be effective in the future and taken into account at the next official negotiation. Therefore, as it often occurs to foreigners, many Japanese are unwilling to officially agree on substantial issues at an early stage of relationship building, and rather leave these important points for a later point in time. [150]

2.1.3.5 Negotiating

Apart from slow decision making processes and unofficial meetings, there are some more aspects to Japanese negotiation style which may strike the Westerner as unusual.

While negotiations in many Western countries are by definition oriented towards achieving tangible result, ideally in the form of a signed agreement,

---

[149] Wichert (2004), p. 1
[150] cf. Wichert (2004), p. 1

the Japanese negotiator has another area of main focus: „Japanese [...] consider that the immediate goal of negotiation is not a signed contract but a relationship between the two sides. Although the written contract expresses the relationship, the essence of their deal is the relationship itself."[151] Good and harmonious *ningen kankei* (人間関係, human relations) are the central purpose which is more important than any single issue within the negotiation, and the Japanese will go out of their way to maintain them, even if this means great sacrifice for their company or them personally. [152] Addressing issues directly, especially if one does not know the other's opinion about them yet, is avoided as far as possible as it could cause discord.

Instead of competing for a better position or trying to win concessions from their counterparts, Japanese negotiators will attempt to establish general norms of the target relationship regarding obligations to each other, benevolence, and the appreciation of others' opinion. [153]
If disagreement does arise, an immense pressure lies on Japanese negotiation parties to resolve it by finding a compromise acceptable for both sides, whereat "acceptable" is often stretched to the extreme for the sake of the long-term relationship. [154] Japanese negotiators can display considerable flexibility if need be, allowing the solution to precede the principle. If it becomes obvious that an agreement cannot be reached, the topic is left out altogether, and the next agenda topic is discussed instead.[155]

On the other hand, cases of exactly the opposite behaviour are known to be frequent. Sometimes Japanese negotiation partners seem unreasonably

---

[151] Gaspardo (2000), p. 26
[152] cf. Bifani (2003), p. 1
[153] cf. Herbig et.al., p. 1
[154] cf. Bifani (2003), p. 1
[155] cf. Herbig et.al., p. 1

focussed on small details or technicalities, and regularly this inflexibility is the cause of failure for negotiations. The reason for this course of action may lie in a negative impression the other negotiation party has created, by seeming inflexible or not sufficiently accommodating themselves.[156]
Another possible reason is the difficulty of changing decisions once they have been made within their own organization. Considering the time and effort necessary to prepare a decision (see chapter 2.1.3.4), it may be easier to insist on its acceptance by the negotiation partner.[157]

Still, flexibility is required and practiced in Japan, especially by the negotiating party in the weaker or dependent position. Contracts, as the outcome of negotiations, are not detailed regulations of every main and collateral duty of the parties and of any eventuality that might happen. Rather, they take the form of gentlemen's agreements, merely documenting the nature of the relationship in short and ambiguous wording, expressing mutual trust and goodwill.[158] There is no such thing as fine print, and no clauses regarding violation of contract or possible legal actions, as it is considered inappropriate to discuss the possible failure of a relationship at its very beginning.
If the circumstances under which the contract has been agreed upon change, such general-style formulation allows extensive flexibility, as single items or details can simply be changed by mutual discussions.
Therefore, the Western negotiator should not expect the typical results of a Western style negotiation, especially from the first meetings with his Japanese counterparts. "A business negotiation is a time to develop a business relationship with the goal of long-term mutual benefit. The

---

[156] cf. Bifani (2003), p.1
[157] cf. Herbig et.al, p. 1
[158] cf. Herbig et.al., p. 1

economic issues are the context, not the content, of the talks."[159] First meetings are mainly for gathering information, which is taken back to one's group for analysis and consideration, before making an offer corresponding to what the other side wants as much as possible.[160]

> "The Japanese tend to offer a proposal that approximates their needs and then resist adjusting it. If the initial trust building were carried out successfully, cost may not be bargained on at all. They offer what they feel is correct, proper, and reasonable. The Japanese tend not to ask for much more than they expect to get."[161]

It is easy to see that the tough, confrontation oriented negotiation approach practiced in many Western countries is not appropriate when dealing with a Japanese negotiation partner. Neither should one expect quick results in written form. The one benefit one can anticipate from such negotiations however is the opportunity to obtain and share information.[162] It is expected from the negotiation partner to ask for details, to find out as much as possible about their counterpart, just as the Japanese do themselves. The information obtained in this way can be the basis to build a stable relationship on.

2.1.3.6 Legal conception and conflict solving

Modern Japanese law has mostly been established within the last century, based to a great extent on Western legislation. Early in the 19th century, German and French codices were adopted which had just been developed or come into effect at that time, mainly in the area of civil and commercial law. After World War II, major reforms of the constitution and criminal law as

---

[159] Herbig et.al., p. 1
[160] cf. Herbig et.al., p. 1
[161] Herbig et.al., p.1
[162] cf. Gaspardo (2000), p. 15

well as corporate law were undertaken, with the US constitution and system as a model.

It is safe to say that the West has had a great influence on the Japanese legal system. However, even though the Western businessman will find many familiar concepts in Japanese law, there are considerable differences in how it is actually applied.

While Western legal thinking and theory is based on the idea of rights and duties of a free and autonomous individual, the basis of Japanese legal conception is directed towards the well-being of the group, whose needs prevail over those of the individual.[163]

As described in chapter 2.1.1.2, the conception of what is right and just is not based on guilt, but on a sense of shame. There is no higher entity nor moral power controlling one's conscience. An infringement of rules that goes unnoticed does not burden the offender. If it is noticed and becomes public however, he has brought shame on his family, his company or his country, and must be atoned.[164]

In many cases, the centre of the appropriate atonement is an apology, which is also regarded as part of the compensation for the offended party. (One can be literally sentenced to writing an apology.[165])

In a collectivist context, apologizing is a vital means of restoring the social harmony that has been breached by the offence committed, which is the basic goal of all legal practice.

An apology will also make it possible for the offender to be re-accepted into the community he has affronted: "He who goes to his knees will be helped up again by the others willingly."[166]

---

[163] cf. Thomas (2001), p. 246
[164] Thomas (2001), p. 247
[165] cf. Thomas (2001), p. 252

Limitation of damage prevails over the principle of punishment; the parties are not seen as opponents, and the legal dispute should help to reconcile them.[167] Formal law suits are generally avoided, as they are considered as a last means after every other attempt of settlement has failed. Taking a case to court means acknowledging that the relationship with the other party is past recovery.

An extrajudicial solution is always to be preferred in business life. Law suits can severely damage the company's reputation; moreover they tend to be extremely protracted.[168]

The Japanese dislike for formalized confrontation in form of legal action is not only shown in their disregard of written contracts, which has already been described in chapter 2.1.3.5. It also becomes evident when looking at the number of persons employed in the legal profession in Japan: the total amount of lawyers, judges, and other legal professionals was 20.730 in 2001, which constitutes a ratio of one legal professional per 6,300 citizens (the US ratio is one per 290 citizens, the French 1,630 citizens, the UK's 710 citizens and the German one 740 citizens per legal professional).[169] This makes legal proceedings in Japan extremely slow, and finding a lawyer very difficult, especially if knowledge of foreign law and English language skills are required.

Some argue that the low number of legal professionals is not the effect but the cause of Japanese reluctance to go to court.[170]

Still, it is advisable to foreigners to adapt to the existing conditions and to try and settle a conflict outside of court. (After all, legal actions are considered harmful to personal relationships in the West too.)

---

[166] Thomas (2001), p. 253
[167] Thomas (2001), pp. 247-249
[168] cf. Großmann (1992), p. 238
[169] cf. Nishiyama (2001), p. 1
[170] cf. Yoshida (2003), p. 1

In most cases, the method of choice to resolve a disagreement is to find a mediator.

Japanese courts offer formal proceedings and personnel for conciliation, the purpose of which according to the Law on Civil Conciliation is "to resolve disputes through the mutual concession of the parties, taking into account actual state of affairs and in accordance with reason".[171] Ideally, however, the mediator should be someone with a good relationship to both parties, who is able to talk to the Japanese party in an informal context, and achieve a compromise acceptable for both sides.

This compromise will never be an all-or-nothing solution, in which one side wins and the other loses. Concessions offered by the Japanese conflict party through the mediator should by all means be accepted. Not only will the mediator lose face if his mediation fails, but it will be extremely difficult to achieve a more favourable solution in a court, especially if one is in a dependency situation from the Japanese partner.[172]

Mediation is not only used in large-scale conflicts which might be settled in court in the West, but also for less substantial personal discord.

Conflicts within a group (e.g. among employees of a company), once they become known to the other group members, will often start an informal process similar to the decision making preparation process described in chapter 2.1.3.4. All group members who are in any way connected to the problem will be involved, the problem will be identified and discussed (informally and often in private), and the appropriate countermeasures will be taken, regardless of time and resources needed.[173]

---

[171] Yoshida (2003), p. 1
[172] cf. Thomas (2001), p. 251
[173] cf. Gundling (1999), p. 21

At the source of a conflict between Western and Japanese employees of the same company, there is often the fundamental difference in the conception of "feedback". While in the West it is regarded as honest and decent to speak to someone directly if one thinks that his behaviour is causing trouble, this would never occur to a Japanese, as it would cause loss of face for both parties. Instead, the Japanese will involve a third party and ask them to intervene. Unfortunately, this third party frequently is a common superior, which will create the suspicion in the Westerner that the Japanese wants to cause him trouble.[174]

Thus the attempt to solve a conflict can in fact have the reverse effect and cause another, often more personal conflict.

It takes a lot of cultural sensitivity and awareness to accept such behaviour, which is totally contradictory to one's own values, and to remain constructive in the face of what one would consider betrayal at home. However, one should keep in mind that it may be equally hard for the Japanese to tolerate one's own culturally determined direct and outspoken behaviour.

In the following, real life examples will be described to illustrate how the cultural differences identified above can result in misunderstandings and conflicts.

---

[174] cf. Gundling (1999), p. 21

2.2 Case Studies

2.2.1 Penetrating group structures

The first case study shows just how difficult it can be to penetrate cohesive Japanese group structures, and how culturally insensitive behaviour can result in consolidating one's status as an outsider.

Situation

A large German company in the service industry wanted to enter the Japanese market. As a strategy, they chose to start a partnership with a market leading Japanese company in the same area of business first, to have the opportunity to explore the market, get to know its participants and conditions, and gradually build relationships with various parties who would be important for doing business in Japan. The long-term goal was to establish their own subsidiary in Tokyo.

The liaison office which was opened as a first step was located at the office of their Japanese partner company, and staffed with one German manager, two Japanese employees and some German interns. At first, their activities mainly consisted in market research and providing services to the Japanese subsidiaries of their German customers.

At the same time, the German manager was trying hard to establish business relationships with important potential Japanese customers, making use of the contacts and connections the Japanese partner company provided.

After three years, the German management decided that it was time to increase the level of activities in Japan, and as there was no big progress being reported back from Tokyo, one of the members of the board announced that he would visit the liaison office himself to see how things were going. He requested the liaison office manager to arrange meetings with managers of potential customer and partner companies, as he was convinced that a visit from a board member would make clear the importance the German company attached to the Japanese market, and would actually speed up the closing of business.

The German manager tried to convince him that things would not work in Japan as they worked in Germany, but did not have any success, and was left with no choice but to arrange some visits with the help of his Japanese contacts.

The visits took place as requested by the German member of the board, but did not produce any results apart from a collection of Japanese business cards. According to the German liaison office manager, many potential customers were annoyed with him for wasting their time with, in their eyes, pointless or obtrusive meetings.

What was even worse, the Japanese partner company, through their connections to the visited companies, became aware of the German company's plans to establish an independent subsidiary, and the trust between the partners was severely damaged.

"In the three days of his visit", the liaison office manager complained, "the board member has spoiled three years of hard work."

It took the company two more years before an independent subsidiary could finally be established.

Analysis

The German board member ignored the strong and cohesive group structure existing in Japan, and the strict division in *uchi* and *soto* (insiders and outsiders). Even among Japanese companies, when starting new business relationships, usually a reference is made by a third party who is known to both business partners to some degree.

Trying to get into contact without the necessary context and preparation was bound to fail from the beginning. The ingroup which the board member (and the whole company) was trying to enter, i.e. the total of companies providing and customers demanding the services the German company offered, was obviously very closely linked. Informal information channels spread the news of the board member's visit and its purpose quickly, so they eventually reached the partner company. By not listening to the liaison office manager, who had years of experience in dealing with the Japanese, the board member obviously caused a lot of damage. Needless to say how much money was wasted over the next two years trying to repair the harm and not being able to do business with potential Japanese customers.

2.2.2 Relationship orientation versus uncertainty avoidance

This case study is an example of how inevitably a cross-cultural communication problem becomes a personal problem, which may cause eventually damage to a personal relationship and make it impossible to resolve the merely culture-based differences.

Situation

A Japanese company had acquired a European company to facilitate their European market entry. After some restructuring and hiring a new manager, they started selling their products in Europe through their new subsidiaries.

Sales was going slower than expected, and especially in Germany, revenues were quite unsatisfactory.

The sales force had to deliver a quarterly forecast of expected revenues. Gradually, the requirements towards these forecasts were increased by the Japanese management. The sales representatives had to add more and more detailed data, some of which could only be obtained by guesswork. At some point, they had to update their forecast on a monthly basis.

Still, some of the expected orders did not come in at the expected and forecasted time.

The Japanese manager frequently visited the German subsidiary, and made a habit of calling a sales meeting whenever he was there. At every meeting, there were discussions about the forecast, and regularly, the Japanese manager would get angry and impose new regulations and requirements, and not listen to any explanations or excuses the sales force offered.

The German sales manager tried to mediate, but talking to the Japanese manager alone was even worse. Whenever he tried to explain that some factors in the sales of the product could not be predicted, and that his sales force was motivated and doing the best they could, the Japanese would get even angrier, and would eventually leave the room, sometimes even break off his visit to the subsidiary. "I want a scientific forecast", he regularly told the sales manager.

The German manager, trying to get to the root of the problem, started reading about the Japanese business culture. What he found out was that the Japanese were less legalistic than the average Westerner, didn't place as much emphasis on written contracts, and in negotiations often preferred a less profitable option which was better for the relationship of the parties over a large but short-term profit. His findings left him more confused than before, and he decided that it must be a personal problem of the Japanese manager, which didn't improve the relationship between them at all.

After two years of struggle, the sales manager left the company in frustration. In the meantime, revenues had started increasing, the products gradually becoming known in the European market and marketing measures and sales efforts taking effect. Still, orders were slipping to the next quarter sometimes, or even not be placed at all, contrary to what had been forecasted. And still the relationship between the German sales manager and sales force on the one hand, and the Japanese manager on the other had been very tense, the atmosphere remaining distrustful.

Shortly after the sales manager had resigned, the Japanese manager was reassigned to a position in Japan, and a new Japanese manager came to Europe.

Revenue figures were more satisfactory by now, and an upward trend was showing. So the new Japanese manager did not insist on a "scientific forecast", as his predecessor had called it, and did not get half as angry if an order was delayed as the previous manager had. The atmosphere during his visits was much more relaxed, and while still insisting on an up-to-date forecast, he placed considerably less emphasis on it. The new German sales manager never had any problems getting along with him.

Analysis

The Japanese manager had never managed a whole subsidiary by himself, let alone a multitude of them in different countries. Nor did he have much international experience, and the assignment removed him from his familiar Japanese context and code of conduct. This and the fact that he was under high pressure to succeed obviously amplified his need for uncertainty avoidance, eventually allowing it to prevail over relationship orientation. He resorted to a behaviour that was contradictory to the usual Japanese disregard for written contracts, and demanded to have everything in writing and in extreme detail, trying to reduce uncertainty by obtaining as much information as possible.

The German sales manager, when his team was criticised, did what would be expected from any good team leader in the West: he defended his subordinates. The Japanese, who most certainly expected an apology and the promise to try even harder, was appalled by the sales manager's defiant refusal to take responsibility, as he perceived it.

The problem, which had at first been an intercultural one, eventually developed into a personal problem between the Japanese manager and the German sales manager, which grew to an extent that it could not be resolved even after the causes had been taken away.

2.2.3 Consideration interpreted as criticism

The following example illustrates how trying to be considerate can harm a relationship rather than having a positive effect.

Situation

A large German company in the service industry wanted to establish a subsidiary in Japan. After exploring several possibilities for entering the market, they decided for a partnership with a market leading Japanese company in the same industry.

The Japanese company provided them with some office space and a Japanese secretary who shared her working time between the two companies. Otherwise, there was only German staff. After a while, the German manager decided to hire another Japanese person.

The Japanese company assisted in the recruiting process, and eventually a German-speaking Japanese freshman was hired. She had studied German at university, had spent several months in Germany, and was very motivated to work for a German company. To one of her German colleagues, she mentioned that she was "too direct" for many Japanese people, and that she was glad to work in a non-Japanese environment.

She started work together with about 100 freshmen newly employed by the Japanese partner company. She attended a special training course together with them provided by the Japanese company, to learn about the basics of the business the company was in, and some standard office procedures.

After two weeks, she had her first day in the German office. One of the first tasks she was assigned was writing an invitation letter to a small conference to Japanese customers.

A Japanese business letter is considerably more complicated to write than an English, German or even French one, and the language which is supposed to be employed has almost nothing in common with language used in everyday conversation, private letters, or university papers. Many native Japanese speakers claim to have difficulties with finding the right level of politeness, and so did she. After taking all day, and frequently consulting the Japanese part-time secretary in the morning, she still had not finished the letter by 5 p.m.

Her German boss had an evening appointment with a customer and wanted to leave the office. The other German employees were about to leave too. He didn't want the Japanese employee to work overtime on her first day all alone in the office, so he told her to go home and have the Japanese secretary help her finish the invitation first thing next morning.

Even before he had finished speaking, he realized that he had obviously offended her. He asked one of the German employees with whom the Japanese employee was getting along well to find out what was wrong and to repair the damage if possible.

As soon as the boss had left, the Japanese employee started crying. She felt deeply humiliated by her boss, who obviously thought nothing of her work, and didn't have enough confidence in her that she could finish the task he had assigned to her. Even after the German employee explained that the boss was fully aware of how difficult the task was, and that he had only wanted her not to work so hard on her first day, actually trying to be nice to her, she was still inconsolable, and said she didn't know how to talk to her boss ever again without feeling shame.

At the first opportunity, she applied for a position in Germany at the same company, and left the Japanese subsidiary about nine months after she had started working there.

Analysis

In the collectivist, relationship oriented Japanese society, direct criticism is avoided, especially in front of others. Feedback is almost always provided indirectly, either through a third party, or through subtle comments or actions which can be interpreted as criticism. By taking her first task away from her, not giving her the opportunity to finish it successfully, and assigning it to a seemingly more competent person, the German superior could not have made a clearer statement that he was not satisfied with her work.

Instead of practicing *onjōshugi*, i.e. being lenient towards his employee, the boss had expressed that he had no faith in her performance.

Making matters even worse, the Japanese part-time secretary had witnessed the scene, further contributing to the new employees humiliation.

What makes this misunderstanding even more striking is that the Japanese employee had studied a foreign culture for four years at university. In fact, she said that she was particularly happy to work for a German company rather than for a Japanese one, as many of her friends kept telling her she was too direct and outspoken for a Japanese.

2.2.4 Conflict management

The miscommunication which is at the root of this example's conflict was continuously happening over a long period of time, and escalated because none of the parties involved was able to interpret the other's course of action correctly.

Situation

A Japanese company with subsidiaries in Europe and the USA was introducing a new product line (consisting of software and services) to the Western market.

As implementing the product at customer site required a considerable amount of customisation, and sales itself was already a complicated process, a new department was established in Europe, consisting of a product sales manager, two programmers, three engineers and two salesmen, all of them Europeans.

When the first potential customer was identified in Germany, it quickly became clear that an engineer experienced in the implementation of the product was required. The European product manager, a German, contacted the respective Japanese product manager, and after providing an estimate of how much revenue could be generated by the project at the German customer, the Japanese headquarter agreed to assign a Japanese engineer to Germany for a year.

At his first visit to Germany, the Japanese engineer seemed very shy and not at all happy to be sent overseas for such a long time. His superior, however, made it clear that he would not accept a 'no', and that the engineer had no choice but to accept the assignment. After moving to Germany, and growing accustomed to his new environment, he gradually became integrated into the German team, and also developed a very positive relationship with the German product manager.

The project too was going well, and after several months the German customer placed the order; the project workload had become so extensive by that time that two more Japanese engineers were delegated to Germany to help with the implementation.

At some point during the implementation, a problem occurred. The Japanese engineer occasionally mentioned to the German product manager that there might be a delay in the project schedule, but didn't elaborate on any details. The German manager, not realizing that there might be more behind that hint than concern about workload, did not offer any help, but just asked the Japanese engineer to increase his efforts, and to try and make sure everything went smoothly, pointing out how important the project was for the department and the whole company. The Japanese engineer didn't insist.

After several weeks, it became evident to both vendor and customer that the project would be considerably delayed due to the problem that had occurred earlier. Of course, the customer was very upset.

The German product manager called a crisis meeting with the European general manager, who was also a German, and the Japanese engineer.

During this meeting, the Japanese, when questioned what had gone wrong and why he hadn't reported this earlier, was uncommunicative and not very cooperative. Finally, he stated that he was not responsible for what had gone wrong, that he didn't care as this was a European problem and that he hadn't wanted the assignment and the project with that customer in the first place.

The European general manager was furious and ended the meeting. The product manager was at a loss with the Japanese engineer's behaviour, who had so far been working in a very motivated and committed way, and had never before complained openly about being delegated to Germany.

Eventually, the problem with the customer was resolved, but even afterwards, the relationship between the Japanese engineer and the German product manager was strained. At the office, they didn't talk more than necessary; lunch in the office cafeteria, usually an occasion to relax and joke together for all the department, became awkward. Knowing that the product manager too would be present, the Japanese engineer declined all invitations to private entertainments from colleagues of his department, which he had happily attended before.

The tension could only be decreased after a 'neutral' party intervened. Another employee who had a good relationship with both product manager and engineer noticed the stressful atmosphere between the two of them, and privately asked the product manager what had happened. After listening to his point of view, she approached the Japanese and carefully asked if there was something wrong. The Japanese told her what had happened from his perspective, and that he had announced the problem more than once, but had not been listened to. The mediating employee explained that the German product manager might not have understood him, as Germans were used to much more direct communication than the Japanese, and offered to talk to the product manager on the engineer's behalf. After doing so, the relationship improved again, and even after his assignment to Germany ended, the Japanese engineer would keep in touch on a private basis with the German product manager. He is still frequently sent to Germany for several weeks on various project assignments, and so far, no further miscommunication has occurred.

Analysis

Obviously, the Japanese engineer tried to communicate the problem to the German product manager at an early stage. But what he considered to be sufficient warnings, were just very vague statements of overall concern and maybe scepticism to the German. The non-reaction of the German manager to the Japanese's warnings was hard to interpret for the Japanese. Obviously, the German either didn't want to support him for personal reasons, or he had a fallback plan for the project in case of delay. In any case, he felt he had done his due.

When he was accused of having made a mistake in front of the general manager, there was no proper way of dealing with this loss of face. The product manager obviously intended to cause him harm, blaming him for causing a problem that he had actually tried to avert, and which could have been averted, he felt, if only the product manager had reacted to his warning. The Japanese's almost childlike response of "I didn't want all this anyway" was one of extreme disappointment and humiliation at this "betrayal" from a person he had gotten along with so well.

Luckily, this quite severe misunderstanding could be resolved by using a mediator. All it took was listening to each party's point of view and explaining it to the other.

2.2.5 Priority Japan: Product trademarks

The following is another example of the large-scale distinction between ingroups and outgroups, and the high priority given to the former over the latter.

Situation

A Japanese company doing business worldwide was about to introduce a new product to the Western market. The product consisted of software and services, and contained an Internet portal offering several industry-specific functions to companies operating internationally.

A European product manager was assigned, and he notified the Western marketing communications team, so they could start preparing a release campaign. They started developing a catalogue of activities, and in the process, tried to obtain the ".com" Internet domain corresponding to the Japanese portal (whose name was in English, but with the extension ".co.jp"). To their surprise, they found that there was an international company of exactly that name, which was even offering similar products to theirs.

They checked the legal situation, but obviously that company had been in business for a several years, and had registered its name a long time ago.

The marketing team informed the European product manager of the situation, and asked him what to do. They were told to contact the Japanese headquarters directly. One of the marketing team members happened to have met the Japanese manager of the business unit in charge of the product, wrote him an email, explaining what the problem was, and asking for help.

When after two weeks she still didn't have any reply, she contacted the Japanese marketing team. From them, she learned that the product name had been registered in Japan upon product release to the Japanese market. As the company of that name did not operate in Japan, there had been no problems. No further activities had been undertaken to obtain a trademark even though it had been clear from the start that the product was to be released worldwide. Upon inquiry, she was told that this was the case for all their products, some of which had been introduced to the Japanese market years after the company had started doing business internationally.

Alarmed, the Western marketing team did some more research, and found out that three other products had names that already existed elsewhere, one more of them even in a related industry.

The marketing team undertook several more attempts to obtain help from Japan, but the only way to resolve the problem would have been to rename the product which by then was in use by approximately 20.000 Japanese customers. It seemed impossible to obtain any statement from the business unit manager, and the Japanese marketing team referred the Western marketing team back to the European product managers.

The product, supposed to be a platform for global companies for facilitating information exchange between manufacturers, suppliers, service bureaus and industry experts worldwide (the unique sales proposition being that everything could be done from one single point of entry), had to be released to the Western market under a different name than the one in use in Japan.

Analysis

When the Japanese company had released the portal, they had gone through every procedure necessary for a product release from their point of view. Unfortunately, this point of view did not include any foreign market, so they had only trademarked the name nationally. The Japanese marketing team had focussed on the largest ingroup they belonged to: Japan.

When the Western marketing team member contacted the Japanese product manager, she made two mistakes. First, she directly contacted someone superior to her with whom she had no significant relationship, without trying to find someone with good contacts to him who could have influenced him in a favourable direction. Second, her alarmed email could very well be interpreted as direct criticism, which obviously offended the product manager to the extent that he didn't answer at all.

This could have been avoided if the marketing team member had known more about the Japanese culture; although in this case it would not have changed the result, as the trademark for the product name was already taken in the West.

2.2.6 Saying "yes, but…" instead of "no"

The following case study is an extreme example of what lengths the Japanese may go to and what resources they can be prepared to spend, just to avoid direct rejection or saying no.

Situation

A Japan expert from Germany was working at a Japanese company and simultaneously obtaining a degree in international marketing. Towards the end of her studies, she received a call from a recruiting agent who told her he was looking for a marketing expert with Japanese language skills. The position to be filled was at the German subsidiary of a large Japanese automotive corporation, which had been in the German market for a long time, but was just building a new branch of business globally. For this new line of business, they were looking for a PR manager.

The German expert was interested, and sent a written application, and an interview took place at the recruiting agency (not involving anyone from the company). Both seemed to meet with interest at the German subsidiary. They told the recruiter that they would like to meet the candidate, and he started arranging for an interview at their office.

But before a date for the meeting could be agreed on, the German subsidiary informed the recruiter that the interview would have to take place at the headquarters in Japan.

Both the recruiter and the candidate were a little surprised, as the position was located in Germany, and a flight to Japan plus accommodation would incur considerably higher cost than a one-day trip to the German subsidiary (around 2.000 EUR compared to around 200 EUR). Moreover, the travel costs to Japan might be saved altogether if at an interview with the German management the candidate might be found unsuitable.

Still, preparations were made for a trip to Japan. But again, they were interrupted by a call from the German subsidiary. By now, the German manager sounded just as astonished as the recruiter and the candidate felt. The Japanese management wanted the German subsidiary to pay for the travel cost of the candidate to Japan.

The German subsidiary asked the recruiter to postpone the interview until he had clarified the situation with Japan.

These negotiations turned out to be fruitless. Japan insisted on seeing the candidate first, and having Germany pay for the trip. Germany didn't see the logic behind this, and refused to bear the travel expenses.

After several weeks, the German subsidiary gave up and cancelled the contract with the recruiter, and the vacancy was never filled.

Analysis

The course of action of the Japanese headquarters seems hard to comprehend to Western economic thinking. It become explicable though if one assumes that they never intended to hire a German for the position in question, or never intended to fill the vacancy at all.

Instead of declining their subsidiaries request to recruit someone directly, they set conditions, which gradually became more and more disproportionate. Maybe even the requirement that the candidate speak fluent Japanese was such an intended obstacle. Once the subsidiary had found someone fulfilling the unlikely condition of being a marketing expert and speaking Japanese, another reason to avoid hiring someone had to be found. Hence the request to speak to the candidate first in Japan. When the subsidiary still didn't get the hint and agreed to this, they were asked to pay for an interview they weren't even allowed to take part in.

Only then did the subsidiary suspect that the Japanese behaviour was obviously as direct a no as they could say.

It becomes clear just how intolerable it must be for a Japanese to decline a request directly if one considers the costs incurred by this course of action: Employing a recruiting agency usually costs around 30% of the gross annual salary planned for the vacancy, 1/3 of which is due at the placement of the order, and is not refunded even if no candidate is placed in the job. Obviously, the Japanese were rather prepared to pay a high amount of money than to say "no".

2.2.7 A Japanese management tool in a German organization

This case study is actually not concerned with negotiations between Japanese and Westerners, but describes the attempt to introduce a Japanese management tool into a German organization. It has been included in this book nevertheless, to demonstrate that adapting practices from another culture regardless of the underlying values very often leads to failure rather than success.

Situation

A Japanese corporation had purchased a European company which had been established some 30 years ago, with subsidiaries all over Europe and in the USA. As a large part of the Western employees stayed with the company after the acquisition, the business culture that had grown over the years was, of course, very Western.

Some three years after the acquisition, the German manager of the German subsidiary, who had always been very interested in Japanese management techniques, decided to bring his organization closer to the headquarters' culture, and to adopt some of the management tools in use in Japan. He had read about the Japanese concept of *kaizen* (改善 , lit. continuous improvement) groups, i.e. informal groups of employees meeting after office hours to discuss company problems and come up with solutions or improvement suggestions. This concept seems to work quite well in many large Japanese corporations. Attendance is voluntary, attendees from all hierarchical levels are accepted, and subjects discussed are arbitrary. In some, but not all cases, there is a monetary incentive for improvement suggestions which are implemented in the company. This tool is not so much used for product innovation, as for drawing on the day-to-day experiences of a company's workforce to improve production or administration processes, as well as for quality assurance.

The German manager wanted to introduce this concept to his own organization, but he was aware that he had to adapt it somewhat to make it work in a different cultural context.

At a kickoff meeting involving all employees, groups were put together formally, each consisting of employees from all departments. Each group was assigned a specific task, like analysing the current sales order process for bottlenecks and duplication of efforts, or identifying weaknesses in the company internal communication. Meetings were to take place during office hours, but could be organized at the team's discretion. The deadline for presenting results was set to 6 months from the kickoff meeting.

After 6 months, none of the teams had come up with any results. Some of the teams asked for more time, so the deadline was extended, but still there was no appreciable outcome. It turned out that some of the groups had not had more than two meetings during the whole time.

The German manager did not give up so easily. At the next annual kickoff meeting, he started a second try, with some more adaptations. This time, each team had an official leader, responsible for scheduling meetings and regularly reporting progress to the management. In addition, all employees received a two day training on problem solving and creativity techniques. Again, the deadline for presenting results was set to 6 months later.

This time, the teams met more frequently, but not with much more enthusiasm. Some of the meetings consisted only of the group leader and one more member, the others being busy doing their jobs or having nothing significant to contribute. After 6 months (plus some more delay), a company meeting was held and each group presented the outcome of their meetings. The presentations were more structured and problem solution oriented due to the training, but only two of the 8 groups came up with tangible results.

The project was then altogether abandoned.

Of course, the German manager tried to find out what had gone wrong, and interviewed team leaders and members. It turned out that most employees didn't identify with the tasks they had been assigned to solve, as they didn't feel directly concerned. The service manager's assistant didn't see any benefit in solving a problem which mainly bothered the sales representatives, just as the programmer couldn't think of a reason for spending his time improving an administration process instead of programming software.

The meetings were considered a waste of precious time which could otherwise have been spent getting 'actual work' done.

In addition, the team leaders complained that their authority hadn't been accepted, meeting invitations had been ignored and tasks assigned by them had not been fulfilled on time or not at all. Most team leaders had been chosen from the company's administrative staff, probably on the assumption that what was required from team leaders was mainly organizing skills and experience in setting up meetings. The other intention behind this choice of leaders may have been to give them a chance to contribute more to the company and to take a more active and influencing part within the organization.

The downside of this was that almost all team leaders were from a low hierarchical level, and were not taken seriously.

Analysis

As described above, the Japanese take a much more holistic view to the world than the average Westerner. An improvement of a part, however small, contributes to the improvement of the whole, and constitutes a benefit for the group (in this case the company). In a collectivist culture, this benefit alone may serve as a large motivator for investing personal effort and time.

In the much more individualist West, even in Germany, which scores only 7 ranks higher on the individualism list than Japan, it often takes a more direct incentive for putting extra effort into a task which holds no intrinsic motivation. This difference had been overlooked by the German manager, as well as the fact that specialization was much higher in his subsidiary than in an average Japanese organization, where basically everyone is trained to be able to do everything. Thus, most Japanese employees learn to understand the needs and problems of every department of their company, and their relevance to the whole organization. Especially highly specialized experts in a German organization often lack this understanding, and thus are not motivated to solve "other people's problems".

2.2.8 Expressing individual opinion

The following case study can almost be considered a textbook example of negotiation differences between members of an individualistic and a collectivistic culture. It will also demonstrate that only one person not aware of cultural differences can cause considerable difficulty even if all other parties in the negotiation are culturally sensitive.

Situation

Company J, a large Japanese company doing business worldwide had acquired a European company of the same industry some 10 years ago. With the purchase, among other things, they inherited some partnerships the European company had established. One of them was with a smaller US-American company (Company A) specializing in products complementary to some of the product lines of Company J, respectively the former European company. Although loose contact was maintained throughout the years with Company A from the European and American subsidiaries of Company J, there were no efforts to update or re-negotiate the partnership from the Japanese side. After a meeting at an industry tradeshow in the US, the American General Manager of Company J suggested to the (also American) General Manager of Company A that he present his company and products to the Japanese management.

The manager of Company A decided that during his next business trip to Japan, where the company already had some customers, would be a suitable occasion, and contacted the headquarters of Company J to set up a meeting with the manager in charge of the concerned product line.

During the time in which the meeting was scheduled, three Western employees of Company J happened to be at the Japanese headquarters: one engineer from the United Kingdom, one from Germany, and one German interpreter. They were asked by an employee of the department in charge of the concerned product line. As they knew Company A and were familiar with the partnership existing in the West, they were eager to attend and support the GM of Company A, knowing that Company A had valuable contributions to make to the product line.

They were surprised, however, when on the day of the meeting, the Japanese product manager, who would have been the appropriate discussion partner for the subject, announced that he had no time to attend, and sent only one engineer from his department in his stead. This was all the more astonishing, as it was going to be an all day meeting at the headquarters of Company J, so he could surely at least have taken the time to welcome Company A's GM, talk to him during a break in the meeting, or have a quick lunch in the office's cafeteria.

Nevertheless, the meeting was held as planned, Company A's GM presenting his company, business plan, products and possible co-operation strategies, all very convincing and obviously beneficial for both sides.

After the presentations and product demos were finished, and some questions, mostly supplied by the Western engineers, were answered, the American GM carefully asked how the presentation was received, and what was the impression on the Japanese side.

The Japanese engineer made some general comments on how interesting the information provided was, but wouldn't give any clear opinion or even an overall tendency for or against a partnership.

The English engineer, already enraged by the fact that the product manager was not present, and wanting to support Company A, tried rephrasing the question several times, to get an opinion out of the Japanese engineer. Finally, after several more vague and polite answers signifying nothing, he directly asked the Japanese engineer to forget about the company for a moment and state his personal opinion about what he had seen.

The Japanese, at first, didn't reply at all, and after several moments of silence, asked the interpreter what the Englishman had said, although his English had clearly been good enough to understand most of the dialogue before. After having the question translated into Japanese, he answered in Japanese that he would have to consult his boss first.

Sensing the awkwardness of the situation, the interpreter tried to explain to the Western attendees that it would be best to end the meeting here and to get in contact again once the situation had been discussed internally.

Company A's GM left Company J's headquarters without any tangible results, and feeling that he had wasted a whole day convincing someone who did not have any influence within his company.

Analysis

The American GM, being signalled interest from the US subsidiary of Company J, was assuming that this interest would also exist in Japan. He obviously didn't think it would be necessary to use Company J's US subsidiary as a supporter of his case. So his call to the Japanese headquarter came unexpected to the Japanese product manager, who couldn't assess the caller's position, social rank, and trustworthiness. The American GM remained an outsider with no relation to any group in Japan, and thus of no interest to the Japanese product manager. He was treated accordingly, although in the typical, subtle Japanese way: the product manager pretended to be not available, which would have been perceived as a direct rejection, if not insult, by a Japanese negotiation partner.

Not realizing this, the American accepted the alibi-attendee who had been sent to the meeting to represent Company J, and carried on with his plans.

When asked to state his individual opinion, the Japanese, who had obviously not been prepared for negotiating any issues during the meeting (see chapter 2.1.3.5), was greatly embarrassed. Admitting that he had no idea if Company J was interested in a partnership or not would have meant a loss of face both for him and the American guest. Stating his personal opinion on Company A's product would mean risking not to be consistent with his company's official position, and equally result in loss of face.

He resorted to the only visible exit out of this awkward situation, pretending not to understand the question and letting someone else repeat what he had already said: that he was in no position to give an opinion.

The interpreter was well aware of the situation. However, if she had tried to explain to the American what the problem was, she would have had to do so in English, which she knew the Japanese still understood perfectly well. This would likely have caused even more embarrassment, so all she could do was persuade the parties to end the meeting, and explain to the Westerners later in private what had happened.

2.2.9 Possible to know is need to know

This case study, again, shows how behaviour can be interpreted completely contrary to its intended meaning (or even if it is not meant to signify anything) by members of a different culture.

Situation

A Japanese corporation (Company J) operating globally was holding its annual customer conference in Japan. Recently, a large German based company (Company G) had placed a substantial order with them for a software system to be implemented at their production sites worldwide. Employees of Company G's Japanese subsidiary also attended this user meeting.

One of the presentations at the conference was given by a German engineer. As soon as the presentation was over, he was approached by a Japanese sales representative of Company J, who asked him if he could spare some time to meet with the employees of Company G.

They meet in a separate room, and both the sales representative and Company G's employees, all Japanese, were very secretive about the meeting. Before leading the German into the room, Company J's sales representative informed the German engineer that Company G's headquarter had obviously not informed their Japanese subsidiary about the new system to be implemented, and that their Japanese employees were very worried about this fact, and wanted to obtain any information they could about the whole project.

The German, having been involved in part of the project in Germany, did his best to provide them with general and to his judgement non-confidential information, giving them an overview of what a project like this typically contained, what kind of software could be involved and put to which exact use, and what benefits could be achieved by the implementation of such a system. He also talked about the good personal relationship between Company G and Company J in Germany, and how well the people involved in the project from both sides were getting along. Whenever questions got too detailed, he stated that the project was still in a very early phase, and that these details would have to be established later.

Still, Company G's employees seemed to find the information provided very interesting, and the more they learned, the less tense became the atmosphere of the meeting. Both the sales representative and Company G's employees seemed to find the meeting very satisfactory.

After an hour, Company G's employees left to attend another presentation, asking the German engineer not to disclose to their headquarters that they had met him and talked about this project.

The sales representative thanked his German colleague very much, although it was clear that he could have provided most of the information by himself.

Somewhat confused, the German engineer called the manager of the project in Germany to inform him about what had happened. Having indeed a very good relationship to Company G, the project manager decided to find out what was behind all this.

When he visited Company G the next time, he carefully addressed the subject of how the software system would be implemented worldwide, and if it wouldn't be good to inform everyone involved as early in the project as possible. Company G's reply was that they were planning an official release in the company newsletter, and a company-wide promotion campaign to inform everyone involved, and that they were just waiting for the first phase of the project to be completed, to have some presentable results for the campaign.

Analysis

As stated many times, the Japanese way of communicating is much more subtle and indirect than the Western direct style. Therefore, the Japanese have to be very sensitive to any means of transferring information, be it verbally or through gestures, silence or actions.

The Japanese employees of Company G's subsidiary had learned about the project that would impact their work from the Japanese employees of Company J (which again shows how fast and limitless information travels in Japan). They were certain that their mother company had withholding this information from them would have to mean something. Not sharing information may be interpreted as not trusting someone, or it can imply that the information contains some negative consequences. Therefore, the Japanese employees of Company G were very anxious to learn as much as possible about what they thought their headquarters didn't want them to know.

As in Japan "possible to know" equals "need to know" (see chapter 2.1.2.3), and as there is a much larger tolerance for ambiguous and vague information (as opposed to the Western preference for cold hard facts and thoroughly prepared structured presentations of these), it never occurred to the Japanese that the reason for not sharing the information was merely a matter of project management and trying to be consistent and well-prepared when presenting them. Company G's German project manager, who actually wanted to sell his project as well as possible to every subsidiary, caused a lot of anxiety and doubt among his Japanese "target group".

2.2.10 Politics in business

The following case study is, at least from a Western perspective, a positive example of how one can achieve one's goal through 'playing along with Japanese rules'. The outcome may not have established friendship between the parties involved, but ultimately helped to increase the success of the company concerned by accelerating the market release of a product that would otherwise have been delayed much longer.

Situation

A Japanese company with subsidiaries in the West was holding their annual user conference, where Japanese customers could meet and exchange experiences, obtain information about the latest product developments and industry trends, and get in touch with the company's product development staff. Many of the presentations were held by customers, and this year, a German customer had been invited to Japan to give a presentation about the implementation of a new product at his company.

The customer agreed to come to Japan, but had to cancel his visit last minute due to other obligations. As the Japanese company had already announced 'international speakers' to their customers, they happily accepted the offer of one of their German subsidiary's engineers to jump in, as he would be in Japan during the conference anyway.

This engineers area of expertise was a German-made product not (yet) sold in Japan. In fact, it was competing with a product of the same company which was made in Japan. The German product was clearly superior, but so far, the issue whether or not to release it in Japan had not received any attention from top level management.

Still, as the German engineer was the expert for this product, he prepared a presentation about his area of expertise. The presentation title was included in the conference schedule. However, the Japanese manager of the business unit to which the competing product belonged, who was also in charge of the department organizing the conference, asked to remove the product name from the title. The German complied.

The Japanese manager also asked if the Germans could provide an interpreter, as many of the Japanese customers were not too fluent in English. The German engineer had already planned to bring a Japanese speaking German employee with him, as there were several meetings scheduled with the development department for which he too required an interpreter.

Two weeks before the conference, both arrived in Japan. The presentation was not prepared completely yet, but there was sufficient time in-between the development meetings, both for the engineer to create the presentation slides, and for the interpreter to translate them.

During this time, the Japanese business unit manager frequently dropped by their desks – in fact he had cleared some space for them in his own department's open-plan office – to check how the preparation for the presentation was going. He supplied various helpful comments to the original, and offered to go through the translation with the interpreter once it was finished.

The German engineer mostly complied with his advice, which mainly concerned references to the name of the German products, so that finally, it was not discernible from the slides which of the two competing products was being presented. Still, in the presentation notes, frequent references were made to the product name.

When the Japanese manager realized this, he took on a new strategy. Emphasizing how impressive it would be for the Japanese customers to see a German engineer presenting at their user conference, and the presentation being translated to Japanese by a German interpreter, he suggested that it might be even more striking if the engineer gave the presentation in German. This would give the conference an even more international touch. The interpreter expressed doubts that the German engineer would be inclined to speak to his audience in a language that almost certainly nobody could understand. But the business unit manager said that this idea came from the president of the company himself, in other words, should be carried out under all circumstances. So the German engineer agreed to speak in German, but to keep the slides in English, so that at least the audience could understand the visuals and handouts by themselves if they spoke any English.

When the preparation of the presentation was almost finished, the German decided to include a video demonstration of the product in action. In the video, of course, the product with its logo and name was always visible.

The Japanese manager was clearly not happy with this. While praising the quality of the presentation, and expressing how grateful he was that the German engineer had jumped in last minute, he asked both engineer and interpreter to make absolutely sure their presentation would not be too long, as the conference schedule was minutely planned, and customers would get upset if they missed the beginning of the following presentations. At various occasions, he suggested that it would be easy to shorten the presentation just by taking the video out. Also, when the interpreter asked him to go through her translation of the text accompanying the video, he didn't have time for her.

The German engineer, by now very aware of what was going on, made a point of going through the whole presentation including the video and the interpretation and taking the time, just to prove it would not be too long. After finding out that it was actually 12 minutes shorter than the time available, he assured the Japanese manager that they would be on schedule and even have time for questions.

After that, the business unit manager did not make any more change requests to the engineer or the interpreter.

The presentation was held including the video, and met with great interest by the customers.

Only half a year later the product was sold to the first Japanese customer, having been localized and integrated with other Japanese products in a very short timeframe by the Japanese business unit manager's department.

Analysis

Again, the Japanese negotiation partner used the tactics of setting conditions instead of declining a request directly, just like in chapter 2.2.6. But instead of giving up after realizing that these conditions were aimed at keeping him from presenting his product, or starting an open argument, the Western engineer simply said yes to every of the Japanese business unit manager's requests. Thus, he brought himself into a position where the business unit manager was obliged to him by *giri* (see chapter 2.1.3.2). When at the last minute he announced that he would include the video, it was very difficult for the Japanese product manager to take any action against this at all. Still, even after the Westerner had proved wrong his argument that the presentation would take to long, the Japanese couldn't bring himself to oppose the presentation directly.

As soon as the customer's interest was raised, there was nothing the Japanese business unit manager could do to keep a product obviously demanded by Japanese customers from the market. As explained in chapter 1.3 ,"the customer is god in Japan", thus a request from a customer cannot easily be declined. Therefore every effort was made to localize the product quickly, and the business unit manager ceased putting up any resistance.

2.2.11 Foreigners and in-groups

This case study, too, is not truly an example for negotiations, as for the parties involved there was no explicit or immediate target to be achieved by the communication that took place. However, this case shows that it is not impossible for a foreigner to penetrate the seemingly impervious borders of even such an intimate ingroup as a family.

Situation

A German student of Japanese was spending her holidays living with a Japanese family near Tokyo. She had been staying at the family's house for several weeks, taking part in their activities, preparing meals with them and helping with all household tasks, accompanying their children to school and spending their leisure time with them. During the mornings, she was taking Japanese lessons at a local language school.

One afternoon, another German student taking part in the same homestay programme and attending the same Japanese classes was visiting her at her host family's house.

The visiting student was treated with great respect: tea was served in the family's living room, not in the kitchen as usual, and special beautiful teacups were used which the student staying with the family had never seen.

During conversation over tea, the mother of the Japanese family mentioned how much better the visiting student's Japanese was, and that their homestay guest was surely happy to have such a good student as a friend.

Both students were taken aback, and the student living with the family felt hurt that she was obviously considered less capable than her visitor. From someone whom she knew to be extremely polite even by Japanese standards, this statement was all the more surprising and offending.

Analysis

Both students decided to ask a Japanese person for clarification. They described what had happened to their Japanese teacher. He explained to them that by praising an external visitor, and decrying the efforts of the homestay guest, the Japanese mother had acted as if the student was one of her own family. In the hierarchical Japanese society, modesty in the face of "superiors" is absolutely mandatory. The Japanese language reflects this very clearly: the more polite one expresses oneself, the more humble are the words used for everything related to oneself and one's ingroup.

As an external visitor (notably with an existing relationship to the family through the homestay student), the German student not staying at the family had to be treated with the appropriate politeness. Consequently, the host family's mother praised her Japanese language skills and at the same time humbled her homestay guest's ability, just as she would have done with her own children. In fact, the supposed "insult" came close to a (maybe only semi-conscious) adoption into the family.

3 Conclusion
3.1 Coping with cultural differences

The last case study has shown that even though the Japanese society seems impenetrable to foreigners, and even though considerable cultural differences exist, it is not impossible to achieve a certain degree of integration. And integration into at least one or two ingroups in Japan does facilitate communication and negotiation greatly. Even if the negotiation does not take place in Japan, establishing a certain understanding or common ground with one's negotiation partner is crucial to success.

This usually requires good interpersonal skills in a negotiator even in non-international negotiations; when the negotiation partner is from a foreign culture, increased sensitivity and care need to be applied.

Fortunately, intercultural skills can be learned and successfully practiced, if one observes certain basics.

The precondition of understanding a foreign culture is understanding one's own.

> "Selecting the most effective option(s) for a given cross-cultural situation can be tricky because it depends in part on the individual's awareness and understanding of his own "cultural rules". This is not as obvious as it first seems, in much the same way that native speakers of a language are typically hard-pressed to explain their own grammar rules to foreigners. It is a common misconception [...] to aim primarily to get to know other cultures, when in fact developing intercultural communication competence depends first on one's understanding of one's own."[175]

Once one has gained a certain awareness of one's own cultural peculiarities, it is necessary to consciously recognize the other culture's standards and rules, and the way they influence its members' behaviour. Realizing

---

[175] Petersen (2004), p. 26

differences seems easy enough to do. However, when it comes to accepting behaviour that violates one's own cultural values, it often takes a conscious effort not to feel offended and to accept that neither the Japanese interaction partner's character nor his culture is flawed. As stated in the introduction of this book, the difficulty is not to learn certain rituals and symbols through which cultural values are expressed, but to recognize and acknowledge that these values allow and require a specific behaviour which might not be acceptable in one's home culture.

The important thing in intercultural encounters is not to judge: it is essential that one meets the communication partner's values with respect. Value systems, rules on how to treat other people, on how to handle different situations and how to solve conflicts, have developed in every culture, more or less in parallel, and they seem to work for any culture's members if they are among themselves. Therefore, no culture should be considered superior or inferior to another.

This does not mean that the negotiator should change his own value system. "Successful intercultural encounters presuppose that the partners believe in their own values. If not, they have become alienated persons, lacking a sense of identity."[176] The phenomenon of over-adaptation in order to cope with cultural differences is often mockingly termed "tatamization" by expatriates in Japan, alluding to the typical Japanese straw floor coverings called *tatami*. Case study 7 has clearly shown that uncritically adopting other cultures' principles is not recommendable.

On the other hand, the negotiator should not resist being interculturally sensitive for fear of losing his own values: "Cultural relativism does not imply normlessness for oneself, nor for one's society. It does call for

---

[176] Hofstede (2003), p. 237

suspending judgement when dealing with groups or societies different from one's own."[177]

Trying to change one's own value system to match a foreign culture would be just as disastrous as attempting to change the others' cultural standards. To alter collective values of adult people in any intended direction is extremely difficult (even supposing people's assent). Social values can change, but usually not due to someone consciously initiating and directing the modification. What can be changed, however, are practices, both one's own and the others. [178] Especially if one has one common goal, extensive information and communication, increasing experience with members of the foreign culture, and the acceptance of the fact that one's own values are not the absolute and ultimate standards for everything, can lead to a learning process on both sides of the negotiation table, eventually resulting in a mutual convergence.

In any case, good and extensive preparation is essential. This can be done in an autodidactic way, by reading books and other materials on the Japanese culture. However, as there are no standard situations with standard solutions in any negotiation, it is more advisable to obtain more than theoretical knowledge. There are practicing techniques like role-playing exercises, or the "culture assimilator training"[179], in which the participants are presented with various critical interaction situations for which they have to find appropriate solutions, including an interpretation of the behaviour of all persons involved.

---

[177] Hofstede (2003), p. 7
[178] cf. Hofstede (2003), p. 199
[179] cf. Thomas, A. (1995), p. 109

Of course, the ideal way to prepare for an intercultural encounter is gathering intercultural experience, by travelling, living and working abroad, and maintaining contacts with members of other cultures.

In the special case of a delegate being sent to Japan, the preparation should not only include himself, but also his interaction partners at home, especially his superiors and any decision makers involved, as their understanding and support is crucial for the delegate's success abroad.[180]

In the case of people from different cultures working for the same organisation, it is important that the organisation provide an environment where they can exist and interact as equals.[181] Any form of discrimination or ethnocentrism is to be avoided strictly, and the corporate culture should promote respect and tolerance.

Generally, when interacting with Japanese negotiation partners for the first time, one should try to be as respectful as possible towards their rules of behaviour. It is always easier to move from formal to informal than vice versa.[182] The thing to remember is, however, that the Japanese are very conscious of cultural differences, even though it may be only of the superficial ones. Many are, in fact, rather proud of the "uniqueness" of their own culture. They expect unfamiliar behaviour from a foreigner in many situations. Therefore, when in doubt how to behave, it is not inappropriate to ask a Japanese person. The occasion for asking should be chosen carefully, to avoid embarrassing someone in front of others. Ideally, this is done in an informal, private context. The answer should be interpreted keeping in mind the Japanese way of avoiding too direct ways of speaking. (Constructive)

---

[180] cf. Hofstede (2003), p. 232
[181] cf. Hofstede (2003), p. 212
[182] cf. Gaspardo (2000), p. 29

criticism may be softened by positive feedback and thus difficult to discern.[183]

On the other hand, the interculturally skilled foreigner can use his knowledge to his advantage and positively surprise his Japanese counterpart with behaviour conforming to their standards. This can happen in a very conscious and visible way (like mentioning one's knowledge of the tea ceremony), or on a more subconscious level, e.g. through informally involving Japanese co-workers into a decision before it is officially made.

In the latter case, it will probably not even occur to the Japanese that the foreigner has adapted to one of his own cultural standards, but it will create a very positive impression of "being a good person" (just like breaking cultural rules often creates the impression of "being a bad person", see above), and help establish a positive relationship.

3.2 Creating cultural synergies

Cultural differences are often seen as barriers to successful business (and other) interaction. Even when overcoming those hurdles, they are still considered as risks and liabilities rather than assets. But there is another dimension to cultural differences which is so far mostly being failed to notice: there are competitive advantages specific to any cultural profile. With good planning and preparation, these can be utilized to one's benefit.

For example, members of a weak uncertainty avoidance culture are more prone to innovative thinking and developing new ideas. On the other hand, they are often not as good at detailed implementation of such ideas as are members of a high uncertainty avoidance culture.[184] So while it may not make sense from an economic point of view to have a research and development

---

[183] cf. Gundling (1999), p. 21
[184] cf. Hofstede (2003), pp.122-123

department in the USA and the corresponding production facilities in Japan (due to high land prices and labour cost), it could still be advantageous to have a Japanese expert plan and implement production in another country.

Another example are the different advantages brought about through variances along the dimension of long-term orientation or Confucian dynamism (see chapter 2.1.1.5):

> "By the middle of the twentieth century the Western concern for truth gradually ceased to be an asset and turned instead into a liability. Science may benefit from analytical thinking, but management and government are based on the art of synthesis. With the results of Western, analytically derived technologies now being freely available, Eastern cultures could start putting these technologies into practice using their own superior synthetic abilities. What is true or who is right is less important that what works and how the efforts of individuals with different thinking patterns can be coordinated towards a common goal. Japanese management, especially with Japanese employees, is famous for this pragmatic synthesis."[185]

So while it would be short-sighted to adopt Japanese management methods without modifying them to the requirements of different cultural background, it is worthwhile to question the routine patterns of management in one's own culture, which often in fact have been adopted from yet another culture:

> "The economic success of the USA [...] has made people in other countries believe that US ideas about management must be superior and therefore should be copied. They forget to ask about the kind of society in which these ideas were developed and applied – *if* they were really applied as the books claimed. Since the late 1960s the same has happened with Japanese ideas."[186]

---

[185] Hofstede (2003), p. 172
[186] Hofstede (2003), pp. 41-42

As in the previous example, one has to take into account all circumstances, both regarding the environmental background and the organization's specific parameters of operation, before trying to take advantage of cultural differences in such a way.

This precaution granted, there are countless possibilities of profiting from cultural differences. It might be beneficial, for example, for a German company to have their customer service employees trained by a Japanese expert in this area, or for a British company to adopt Japanese quality control standards. Hofstede counts among the competitive advantages of a culture with the Japanese's characteristics: discipline (large power distance), employee commitment (collectivism), efficiency (masculinity) and precision (strong uncertainty avoidance), and argues that cultural consideration should definitely be included in strategic enterprise planning.[187]

But there are also benefits to be drawn from intercultural interaction on a more personal level. Learning to analyse and interpret situations and events based on new and unfamiliar paradigms instead of one's own routine patterns greatly enhances personal skills and management qualification.[188] The flexibility and sensitivity one has to apply when managing an intercultural encounter successfully can be invaluable in countless other (not necessarily intercultural) situations. And being aware of one's own values and the fact that others may hold other values and still not be wrong or inferior is a valuable and desirable personal quality to be gained from cross cultural encounters.

---

[187] cf. Hofstede (2003), p. 240
[188] cf. Kühlmann (1995), p. 22

3.3 Summary

For successful negotiation between members of Western cultures and Japanese counterparts, it is crucial that the Western negotiator finds the right balance between independence and adaptation.

Preconditions for achieving an appropriate degree of adaptation are on the one hand the negotiators personal readiness and open-mindedness and on the other hand the amount of information on the Japanese culture that is available to him. Only based on this information will he be able to decide on a case by case basis if and to which extent adaptation is necessary and suitable.

Knowing every element and aspect of a foreign culture and internalising each of its standards and values is virtually impossible, just as it is impossible to always comply with these standards (even for a member of the respective culture). However, the visible effort to learn about the Japanese culture and the display of respect towards Japanese values will be greatly appreciated by the Japanese witnessing them, and thus facilitate interaction and create a positive atmosphere.

For achieving this level of intercultural understanding and competence, two basic requirements need to be fulfilled by the Western business negotiator, which so far seem to be insufficiently considered.

First, the extent of cultural value differences (not just superficial rituals) between the West and Japan and their practical implications must be acknowledged. These differences are often neglected in business life due to the fact that Japan is a modern industrialized nation. Paradoxically, differences are observed in other areas of life, but often without realizing their full impact. Instead of perceiving culture as no more than a decorative accessory to a nation, it is vital to become aware of its powerful influence on every aspect of everyday (and thus also business) life and all human interaction. Secondly, if this fact is recognized, subsequently the need for comprehensive information on the Japanese cultural circumstances and characteristics arises. Acquaintance with these is indispensable for successful interaction and communication with the Japanese.

Unfortunately, when preparing international negotiations, economical and technical considerations are usually in the foreground. Experts in the field of cultural studies are not employed or even considered by most companies. The standard argument against such experts is that they may be competent in the Japanese culture, but not have sufficient knowledge of economic principles and processes.
The potential for a co-operation between business and cultural experts, within which both sides could bring their specific qualifications to the negotiation is widely disregarded so far. Still, synergetic effects of such co-operations of experts could significantly increase the success of intercultural communication and interaction considerably.

Evidently, Japan is a culture which encompasses many aspects totally alien to the average Westerner. Still, it is not as closed to foreigners as it may appear at first glance. The word 'hurdles' has been chosen for the title of this book rather than barriers, as hurdles are something designed to be jumped over, while barriers are designed to keep someone out. Some of the examples above have shown that it is not entirely impossible to overcome these intercultural hurdles. In fact, "barriers [...] in Japan are created not so much by ‚closed doors' as they are by ‚closed minds'."[189]

---

[189] Steinmann et.al. (1992), p. 1010

4 Indices
4.1 Literature

Abe, Takeshi   事務系ホワイトカラーの企業内移動 *Jimukei howaitokarā no kigyōnaiidō* **(Promotion of white collar workers within corporations)**, in: Nihon Rōdo Kenkyū Zasshi Nr. 426 (Sept. 1995), pp. 30-39, Japanese Institute of Labour, Tokyo, 1995

Befu, Harumi   **Japan – An anthropological interpretation**; Tuttle Publishing, Tokyo, 1981

Bifani, Darin   **Win the Battle or Build a Relationship? How Japanese Style Could Help American Negotiators**; in: Business Law Today, Volume 12, Number 5 - May/June 2003, American Bar Association

Bittner, Andreas   **Psychologische Aspekte der Vorbereitung und des Trainings von Fach- und Führungskräften auf einen Auslandseinsatz**; in: Thomas, Alexander: Psychologie interkulturellen Handelns, Hofgrefe Verlag, Göttingen, 1996

Clark, Gregory   **Japanisches Management – Instinkt und Feudalismus als kulturelle Grundlage,** in: Esser/Kobayashi: Kaishain – Personalmanagement in Japan, Verlag für angewandte Psychologie, Göttingen, 1994, pp. 90-99

Dülfer, Eberhard   **Internationales Management in unterschiedlichen Kulturbereichen**; 4th edition, Oldenbourg Verlag, München, 1996

Gaspardo, Dr. Nello	**Cross Cultural Communication and Negotiation Techniques**; University of Applied Sciences, Reutlingen, 2000
Gross, Ames	**Trends in Human Resources Practices in Japan;** in: SHRM International Focus, Society for Human Resource Management, 1998
Großmann, Bernhard	**Rechtlicher Rahmen und wirtschaftliche Bedingungen in Japan für die Tätigkeit deutscher Unternehmen**; in: Kumar/Haussmann: Handbuch der Internationalen Unternehmenstätigkeit, pp. 238-251, C.H. Beck'sche Verlagsbuchhandlung, Munich, 1992
Gullestrup, Hans	**The Complexity of Intercultural Communication in Cross-Cultural Management**; in: Prof. Jens Allwood (editor): Intercultural Communication, issue 6, 2003/2004; http://www.immi.se/intercultural/
Gundling, Ernest	**Communicating with Japanese in Business**; Japan External Trade Organisation (JETRO), Tokyo, 1999
Hamabata, Matthews Masayuki	**Ethnographic Boundaries: Culture, Class and Sexuality in Tokyo**; in Qualitative Sociology 9 (4), Winter 1986, pp. 354 – 369, Human Science Press, New York, 1986
Herbig, Paul; Howard, Carol; Martin, Drew; Borstorff, Pat	**At the Table: Observations on Japanese Negotiation Style**; www.geocities.com/Athens/Delphi/9158/paper64.html

Hofstede, Geert	**Cultures and organizations; Intercultural Cooperation an its Importance for Survival**, Profile Books, London, 2003
Kammel, Andreas; Teichelmann, Dirk	**Internationaler Personaleinsatz;** R. Oldenbourg Verlag, München, Wien, 1994
Kobayashi, Naoya	松下電器の国際教育プログラム (*Matsushita Denki no kokusaikyōiku puroguramu*, **Matsushita Electris' international training programme**), in: Gendai no Esupuri 1992/6, pp. 160-171, Shibundo, Tokyo, 1992
Kodansha International	**Japan – Profile of a Nation**, Kodansha International Ltd., Tokyo, 1994
Kühlmann, Thorsten (editor)	**Mitarbeiterentsendung ins Ausland**; Verlag für Angewandte Psychologie, Göttingen, 1995
Kumar, Brij N.; Haussmann, Helmut	**Handbuch der Internationalen Unternehmenstätigkeit**; C.H. Beck'sche Verlagsbuchhandlung, München, 1992
Kumar, Brij N.; Steinmann, Horst; Dolles, Harald	**Das Management in Niederlassungen deutscher Unternehmen in Japan**; Diskussionsbeitrag Nr. 2, Lehrstuhl für Betriebswirtschaftslehre, Universität Erlangen/Nürnberg, Nürnberg, 1993
Laskowitz, Kate	**Winning Over the Heart and Mind: A Comparison of Japanese and American Conflict Management Processes;** Nineteenth Annual Southern Industrial Relations And Human Resources Conference, Nashville, 1998; www.tech.purdue.edu/orgs/mediate/jpnpaper.htm

MPHPT (Statistical Research and Training Institute)	**Statistical Handbook of Japan 2003 (SHJ)**; Statistical Research and Training Institute, MPHPT, Tokyo, 2003
Nakamura, Yoshio	**Corporate Governance in Japan**; in: Japan Economic Currents No. 11, Aug. 2001, Keizai Koho Center, Japan Institute for Social and Economic Affairs, Washington, 2001
Nakane, Chie	**Die Struktur der japanischen Gesellschaft**, Suhrkamp Verlag, Frankfurt, 1985
Nishiyama, Hidehiko	**Japan's Judiciary Reform**; in: Inside/Outside Japan, vol. 9, March 2001, JETRO, New York, 2001 www.jetro.go.jp/usa/newyork/inside/iomarch2001.html
Petersen, Alexia	**Intercultural Communication Skills: Essential for Today's Global Marketplace**; in: Canadian German Trade, vol. 16/2, March/April 2004, pp. 25-27, Canadian German Chamber of Industry and Commerce www.germanchamber.ca/shared/CGT_art/CGT0402/intercultural.pdf
Pohl, Manfred	**Japan**; 2nd edition, C.H. Beck'sche Verlagsbuchhandlung, München, 1992
Rowland, Diana	**Japan-Knigge für Manager**, Campus Verlag, Frankfurt, New York, 1994
Sakamoto, Yasumi	海外企業経営と現地人 (*Kaigaikigyōkeiei to genchijin*; Local people and the management of foreign companies), Nikkeishinsho, Tokyo, 1976

Schlunze, Rolf D.	**Adjustments of European Management in Japan**, EIBA 2002 Annual Conference, Otemon Gakuin University, Osaka, 2002 www.aueb.gr/deos/EIBA2002.files/PAPERS/C61.pdf
Spieß, Erika	**Kooperatives Handeln in Organisationen**; Theoriestränge und empirische Studien; Mering, München, 1996
Steinmann, Horst; Kumar, Brij; Dolles, Harald	**Eintritts- und Führungsstrategien deutscher Unternehmen in Japan**; in: Kumar/Haussmann: Handbuch der Internationalen Unternehmenstätigkeit, pp. 995 – 1011, C.H.Beck'sche Verlagsbuchhandlung, Munich, 1992
Thomas, Alexander	**Die Vorbereitung von Mitarbeitern für den Auslandseinsatz: Wissenschaftliche Grundlagen**; in: Kühlmann: Mitarbeiterentsendung ins Ausland, pp. 85-118, Verlag für Angewandte Psychologie, Göttingen, 1995
Thomas, Gothild und Kristina	**Reisegast in Japan**; Iwanowski's Reisebuchverlag, Dormagen, 2001
Whitehill, Arthur M.	**Japanese Management – Tradition and transition**; Routledge, London, New York, 1991
Wichert, Robert	**In Search of a Japanese Rhetoric: an alternative view**; 2004; www.wichert.org/icrhetja.htm

Yoshida, Masayuki **The Reluctant Japanese Litigant - A 'New' Assessment;** in: electronic journal of contemporary japanese studies, (Discussion paper 5), Oct. 2003
www.japanesestudies.org.uk/discussionpapers/Yoshida.html

4.2 Index of tables

Table 1: Power Distance Index (PDI) 23
Table 2: Individualism Index (IDV) 26
Table 3: Masculinity Index (MAS) 31
Table 4: Uncertainty Avoidance Index (UAI) 34
Table 5: Long Term Orientation 38

4.3 Index of figures

Figure 1: Total hours worked per annum by country (manufacturing) 57
Figure 2: Decision making and implementation in the US and Japan 65

4.4 Japanese terms

aisoo-warai
愛想笑い laughter of courtesy, civility — 48

giri
義理, duty, sense of duty — 59

henna gaijin
変な外人, strange foreigner — 14

honne
本音, one's true feelings — 62

juku
塾, private coaching school — 52

kaizen
改善, process of continuous improvement — 91

kata
形, the proper form of things — 62

kokusaika
国際化, internationalisation — 8

ningen kankei
人間関係, human relations — 67

on
恩, favour, obligation — 59

onjoushugi
温情主義, paternalism, showing a warm heart — 59

ringi seido
稟議制度, system of reaching a decision via a document circulated to all employees — 64

shiken jigoku
試験地獄, examination hell — 52

soto
外, outside, outgroup — 29

tatemae
建前, the face one shows to the outside world — 62

uchi
内, inside, ingroup — 29

ibidem-Verlag
Melchiorstr. 15
D-70439 Stuttgart

info@ibidem-verlag.de

www.ibidem-verlag.de
www.edition-noema.de
www.autorenbetreuung.de

www.ingramcontent.com/pod-product-compliance
Lightning Source LLC
Chambersburg PA
CBHW070739230426
43669CB00014B/2514